Is It Okay to PRAY in *tongues* in CHURCH?

An in-depth study of 1 Corinthians Chapter 14

BY PASTOR JIM LANGLOIS

Scriptures quotations marked TLB are taken from *The Living Bible* © 1971. Used by permission of Tyndale House Publishers, Inc., Wheaton, Illinois 60189. All rights reserved.

Scripture quotations marked THE MESSAGE are taken from *The Message*, copyright © by Eugene H. Peterson, 1993, 1994, 1995, 1996. Used by permission of NavPress Publishing Group. All rights reserved.

Is it Okay to Pray in Tongues in Church?
ISBN 0-88144-290-9
Copyright © 2008 by Jim Langlois
P.O. Box 1568
Mechanicsville, VA 23116

Printed in the United States of America. All rights reserved under International Copyright Law. Contents and/or cover may not be reproduced in whole or in part in any form without the express written consent of the Author.

TABLE OF CONTENTS

FOREWORD 5

INTRODUCTION 7

   Chapter One:
      An Overview of 1 Corinthians
      Chapters Twelve through Fourteen 9

   Chapter Two:
      Seeker-sensitive or God-sensitive? 13

   Chapter Three:
      Establishing Important Key Truths 25

   Chapter Four:
      It Depends On Who You Are Speaking To! 31

   Chapter Five:
      Why Did God Invent Tongues? 45

   Chapter Six:
      Tongues, a Sign to Unbelievers—
      Not the Message 51

   Chapter Seven:
      The Fifth Key Is "All" 59

   Chapter Eight:
      Can We Only Have Two or Three? 63

   Chapter Nine:
      Can Women Prophesy? 67

Chapter Ten:
    The Sixth Key Is "All Things" 69

Chapter Eleven:
    The Seventh Key Is Love 71

Chapter Twelve:
    New Testament Prayer Meetings 75

Chapter Thirteen:
    What about "Tongues Shall Cease?" 83

Chapter Fourteen:
    How to Be Saved 87

Chapter Fifteen:
    Now Is the Time—
    Be Baptized In the Holy Spirit! 91

Chapter Sixteen:
    Ten Good Reasons to Pray In Tongues 101

Chapter Seventeen:
    Developing Your Prayer Language 105

Chapter Eighteen:
    How to Stay Filled With the Spirit 107

Chapter Nineteen:
    Declaration of Independence 111

CONCLUSION 113

BIBLIOGRAPHY 117

About the Author 119

FOREWORD

The day the first New Testament Church was birthed, heaven exploded upon the earth. One-hundred and twenty lovers of Jesus began speaking in tongues and magnifying God. This was not a secret event. Crowds of people—Jewish pilgrims from near and far—ran towards the commotion. Were they repelled? No! They marveled at what they heard. Did it cause confusion? No! That day three-thousand souls were swept into the Kingdom. It was as Jesus promised, *"You will receive power after that the Holy Ghost is come upon you."*

Countless believers forfeit the blessing of Pentecost because modern preachers seem to think people can't handle the truth. Thus, tongues has been ignored, explained away, or marginalized. However, we have only to read the bible to see that this gift is for us, today.

Pastor Jim Langlois has wrought a great work in his book, *Is it Okay to Pray in Tongues in the Church?* The definitive answer is yes. You will come to the same conclusion as you examine the scriptural proofs and sound arguments put forth by Pastor Jim. Finally, someone has addressed the weak theology of today's hyper-friendly and politically-correct Christian impresarios.

Take this book home, open your bible, and discover for yourself that it's not just okay to pray in tongues in the church—it's vital.

Larry Huggins, D.D.

IS IT OKAY TO PRAY IN TONGUES IN CHURCH?

An in-depth study of 1 Corinthians Chapter 14

Introduction

So he answered and said to me: "This is the word of the Lord to Zerubbabel: 'Not by might nor by power, but by My Spirit,' Says the Lord of hosts" (Zechariah 4:6).

It is not my desire or intent to offend anyone or cause division by this writing, but I am fully aware it may do so. If you will open your heart to the Word and hear "what the Spirit says" I believe it will set you free.

"He who has an ear, let him hear what the Spirit says to the churches" (Revelation 2:29).

If after you read this and you are still in disagreement, I accept your disagreement and have no desire to argue or debate the issue. I will however, say that "these signs shall follow those who believe" (Mark 16:17a).

"IS IT OKAY TO PRAY IN TONGUES IN CHURCH?"

Praying in tongues or not praying in tongues does not have any determination on someone's salvation, righteousness through Christ, or zeal and love for God. It does not make one more spiritual than another; however, it does enable one to be more effective in the realm of the Spirit. It's like having an electric or gas powered tool instead of a manual hand tool. It is the way to go beyond your own human understanding, limitations, and abilities, and to enter into God's Spirit world of omniscience (all-knowledge), omnipresence (all-presence), and omnipotence (all-power), which can only come through God Himself.

My prayer is that as you read this book you will not be offended but rather enlightened and set free to fellowship with God in ways that you never thought possible. It's called "mysteries," a word in the original Greek which is defined as "that which, being outside the range of unassisted natural apprehension, can be made known only by divine revelation, and is made known in a manner and at a time appointed by God, and to those only who are illumined by His Spirit."[1]

> For he who speaks in a tongue does not speak to men but to God, for no one understands him; however, in the spirit he speaks mysteries (1 Corinthians 14:2).

---

[1] Vine, W., Unger, M. F., & White, W. (1997, c1996). *Vine's complete expository dictionary of Old and New Testament words* (electronic ed.) (2:424). Nashville: Thomas Nelson.

CHAPTER ONE:

An Overview of 1 Corinthians Chapters Twelve Through Fourteen

1st CORINTHIANS

Chapter 12 *Need for Variety*		Chapter 13 *Need for Love*		Chapter 14 *Need for Control*	
1-3	Don't be Ignorant				
4-11	Variety in the gifts	1-3	Spiritual gifts without love have no value	1-19	Prophecy preferred before speaking in tongues
12-27	Variety in the body	4-7	The operation of love	20-25	Tongues—as a sign to unbelievers
28-31	The operation of the gifts through the body	8-13	Love is the greatest gift and will never cease	26-40	Order in the church / forbid not to speak in tongues

When studying a Bible scripture or passage it is always best to study in context. This means that you look at the scriptures or chapters previous to and after the passage you are studying, to see if there is a central theme or thought that the writer is trying to convey. Another approach would be to determine the time and place it was written, to see how these may influence the overall theme from a historical or cultural view. As we examine 1 Corinthians, chapter fourteen, it would benefit us to look at chapters twelve and thirteen as they lead up to the conclusions Paul makes in chapter fourteen.

Chapter twelve starts out with Paul telling us not to be ignorant about spiritual gifts. He then proceeds to tell us about the variety of gifts, the variety in the body of Christ (that's us) that the gifts will flow through, and how they should operate through us.

In chapter thirteen Paul emphasizes love, the most important governing factor. Love should be our motivation for the gifts to flow. Then, in detail in chapter fourteen he tells us we must operate these gifts with the benefit of the church as our first priority. There were obviously some problems in the church at that time. Paul's efforts were to bring balance to a situation of imbalance. There was too much "Spirit" and not enough practical benefit for those who were attending the services. He went to great lengths to teach on the difference of prophecy verses tongues, saying that prophecy would be of better benefit because it can be understood by the hearers in four different types of manifestations… revelation, knowledge, prophesying, and teaching. Paul was thankful that he spoke in tongues more than any of them, but if all they do is speak and pray in tongues, no one will understand and benefit from the word of the Lord. Although at that time, the church may have been too tilted toward the spirituality of tongues, Paul is careful to say that as they bring balance between the Spirit and the understanding, they do not go too far the other way and quench the Spirit. Tongues are a sign to the unbeliever; therefore they should not forbid speaking in tongues, but seek for decency and order.

Paul explains three simple truths: one, there is a variety of gifts, bringing the need for a variety of people within the body of Christ for these gifts to operate, two, in order for these gifts to benefit anyone, they must be operated within the parameters of love toward others, and three, there is a need for control to be sure it IS the manifestation of the Spirit of God and not a false manufactured (faked) gift for the purpose of bringing glory to man. The control should seek to excel "the church" as a whole through edification, exhortation and comfort.

"IS IT OKAY TO PRAY IN TONGUES IN CHURCH?"

he ever *not* heal anyone or do miracles in the temple so they would not be offended? Look at one of His discourses...

> 33 But whoever denies Me before men, him I will also deny before My Father who is in heaven.
>
> 34 "Do not think that I came to bring peace on earth. I did not come to bring peace but a sword.
>
> 35 For I have come to 'set a man against his father, a daughter against her mother, and a daughter-in-law against her mother-in-law';
>
> 36 and 'a man's enemies will be those of his own household.'
>
> 37 He who loves father or mother more than Me is not worthy of Me. And he who loves son or daughter more than Me is not worthy of Me.
>
> 38 And he who does not take his cross and follow after Me is not worthy of Me.
>
> 39 He who finds his life will lose it, and he who loses his life for My sake will find it (Matthew 10:33-39).

These may seem like very harsh statements, but they are the truth. Jesus did not let man run the Sabbath services; rather he stated that the Sabbath was to help man, not man to help the Sabbath.

> And He said to them, "The Sabbath was made for man, and not man for the Sabbath (Mark 2:27).

Several other translations help to see the real meaning of Jesus' statement...

CHAPTER TWO

Seeker-Sensitive or God-Sensitive?

This brings us to the question: **Is it ok to pray in tongues in church?** This is a big debate. Some Pastors and Churches are staying away from it because they either do not understand what to do, or they believe the scriptures teach against it.

Some churches have a vision to be "Seeker Sensitive, or Seeker Friendly." This means they do not want to offend anyone by any manifestation of the Holy Spirit and His gifts in the services. In my view, this would water down the power of the Spirit to please people instead of pleasing God.

There are two *possible* definitions (my definitions) of "Seeker Sensitive or Seeker Friendly."

"IS IT OKAY TO PRAY IN TONGUES IN CHURCH?"

1) To tailor a church service so as to attract and not to offend a "Seeker" by conducting the service as follows:

   - not having an altar call (asking for a decision to receive Christ)
   - not talking about hell or condemnation
   - not having a pulpit
   - not preaching from a Bible
   - not having the image of a Cross displayed
   - using secular music and words
   - not having songs about the blood of Jesus
   - keeping the service extremely short
   - not having the Gifts of the Spirit in operation
   - not allowing speaking or singing in other tongues
   - not talking about sin, repentance, or a change of lifestyle
   - not allowing the supernatural in miracles and healing

2) To tailor a church service so as to attract and to minister to a "Seeker" by conducting the service according to Mark 16:15-18.

the supernatural power of healing, faith, and miracles to flow.

- Calling people to repentance, salvation, and the baptism of the Holy Spirit with the evidence of speaking in other tongues.

Why is it that "Seeker Sensitive or Seeker Friendly" means we should water down what God wants to do? Shouldn't "Seeker Sensitive or Seeker Friendly" mean we will offer them what they really need, which is all the power of God? Shouldn't we be "God-sensitive" to what seekers really need? I prefer the term "God Sensitive or God Friendly."

> 7 And as you go, preach, saying, 'The kingdom of heaven is at hand.'
>
> 8 Heal the sick, cleanse the lepers, raise the dead, cast out demons. Freely you have received, freely give (Matthew 10:7-8).

Do we see the early church as "Seeker Sensitive?" Did they design their services and prayer meetings for what would not offend, or do we see them operating as "God Sensitive," allowing freedom for all the power of God to operate? Phillip the evangelist brought great joy to the city of Samaria by obeying the command of Jesus.

> 4 Therefore those who were scattered went everywhere preaching the word.

CHAPTER TWO

Seeker-Sensitive or God-Sensitive?

This brings us to the question: **Is it ok to pray in tongues in church?** This is a big debate. Some Pastors and Churches are staying away from it because they either do not understand what to do, or they believe the scriptures teach against it.

Some churches have a vision to be "Seeker Sensitive, or Seeker Friendly." This means they do not want to offend anyone by any manifestation of the Holy Spirit and His gifts in the services. In my view, this would water down the power of the Spirit to please people instead of pleasing God.

There are two *possible* definitions (my definitions) of "Seeker Sensitive or Seeker Friendly."

"IS IT OKAY TO PRAY IN TONGUES IN CHURCH?"

1) To tailor a church service so as to attract and not to offend a "Seeker" by conducting the service as follows:

- not having an altar call (asking for a decision to receive Christ)
- not talking about hell or condemnation
- not having a pulpit
- not preaching from a Bible
- not having the image of a Cross displayed
- using secular music and words
- not having songs about the blood of Jesus
- keeping the service extremely short
- not having the Gifts of the Spirit in operation
- not allowing speaking or singing in other tongues
- not talking about sin, repentance, or a change of lifestyle
- not allowing the supernatural in miracles and healing

2) To tailor a church service so as to attract and to minister to a "Seeker" by conducting the service according to Mark 16:15-18.

- Teaching and preaching the uncompromised gospel; declaring that those who believe and are baptized into the body of Christ will be saved (Galatians 3:26-27, Ephesians 2:8, 1 Corinthians 12:13), and those who do not believe will be condemned,

- Teaching, preaching, and demonstrating that these signs will follow those who believe... casting out devils, speaking in new tongues, taking up serpents (taking authority over Satan himself), if they accidentally drink anything deadly they will not be hurt, and if they lay hands on the sick they will recover. Going out, with the Lord working through them, preaching everywhere and confirming the Word through the accompanying signs.

- Preaching the Bible definition of sin, repentance, and calling on the name of the Lord to be saved.

- Preaching the reality of God, Jesus Christ, the Holy Spirit, Heaven, Hell, Satan, demons, angels, the Book of Life, and the Great White Throne Judgment.

- Allowing the 9 Gifts of the Spirit to operate, allowing saints to pray and to sing with the understanding and with the spirit, and allowing the supernatural power of healing, faith, and miracles to flow.

- Calling people to repentance, salvation, and the baptism of the Holy Spirit with the evidence of speaking in other tongues.

Why is it that "Seeker Sensitive or Seeker Friendly" means we should water down what God wants to do? Shouldn't "Seeker Sensitive or Seeker Friendly" mean we will offer them what they really need, which is all the power of God? Shouldn't we be "God-sensitive" to what seekers really need? I prefer the term "God Sensitive or God Friendly."

> 7 And as you go, preach, saying, 'The kingdom of heaven is at hand.'
> 8 Heal the sick, cleanse the lepers, raise the dead, cast out demons. Freely you have received, freely give (Matthew 10:7-8).

Do we see the early church as "Seeker Sensitive?" Did they design their services and prayer meetings for what would not offend, or do we see them operating as "God Sensitive," allowing freedom for all the power of God to operate? Phillip the evangelist brought great joy to the city of Samaria by obeying the command of Jesus.

> 4 Therefore those who were scattered went everywhere preaching the word.

"IS IT OKAY TO PRAY IN TONGUES IN CHURCH?"

13 "But woe to you, scribes and Pharisees, hypocrites! For you shut up the kingdom of heaven against men; for you neither go in yourselves, nor do you allow those who are entering to go in.

14 Woe to you, scribes and Pharisees, hypocrites! For you devour widows' houses, and for a pretense make long prayers. Therefore you will receive greater condemnation.

15 "Woe to you, scribes and Pharisees, hypocrites! For you travel land and sea to win one proselyte, and when he is won, you make him twice as much a son of hell as yourselves (Matthew 23:13-15).

23 "Woe to you, scribes and Pharisees, hypocrites! For you pay tithe of mint and anise and cummin, and have neglected the weightier matters of the law: justice and mercy and faith. These you ought to have done, without leaving the others undone.

24 Blind guides, who strain out a gnat and swallow a camel!

25 "Woe to you, scribes and Pharisees, hypocrites! For you cleanse the outside of the cup and dish, but inside they are full of extortion and self-indulgence.

26 Blind Pharisee, first cleanse the inside of the cup and dish, that the outside of them may be clean also.

27 "Woe to you, scribes and Pharisees, hypocrites! For you are like whitewashed tombs which indeed appear beautiful outwardly, but inside are full of dead men's bones and all uncleanness.

5 Then Philip went down to the city of Samaria and preached Christ to them.

6 And the multitudes with one accord heeded the things spoken by Philip, hearing and seeing the miracles which he did.

7 For unclean spirits, crying with a loud voice, came out of many who were possessed; and many who were paralyzed and lame were healed.

8 And there was great joy in that city (Acts 8:4-8).

Paul encourages the church to operate in the power of God rather than in the wisdom of men!

For I am not ashamed of the gospel of Christ, for it is the *power of God* to salvation for everyone who believes, for the Jew first and also for the Greek (Romans 1:16).

For the message of the cross is foolishness to those who are perishing, but to us who are being saved it is the *power of God* (1 Corinthians 1:18).

4 And my speech and my preaching were not with persuasive words of human wisdom, but in *demonstration of the Spirit and of power,*

5 that your faith should not be in the wisdom of men but in the *power of God* (1 Corinthians 2:4-5).

But what about the possibility of offending someone and they leave the church never to return? I would question and say; did Jesus ever water down his message? Did

"IS IT OKAY TO PRAY IN TONGUES IN CHURCH?"

he ever *not* heal anyone or do miracles in the temple so they would not be offended? Look at one of His discourses...

> 33 But whoever denies Me before men, him I will also deny before My Father who is in heaven.
>
> 34 "Do not think that I came to bring peace on earth. I did not come to bring peace but a sword.
>
> 35 For I have come to 'set a man against his father, a daughter against her mother, and a daughter-in-law against her mother-in-law';
>
> 36 and 'a man's enemies will be those of his own household.'
>
> 37 He who loves father or mother more than Me is not worthy of Me. And he who loves son or daughter more than Me is not worthy of Me.
>
> 38 And he who does not take his cross and follow after Me is not worthy of Me.
>
> 39 He who finds his life will lose it, and he who loses his life for My sake will find it (Matthew 10:33-39).

These may seem like very harsh statements, but they are the truth. Jesus did not let man run the Sabbath services; rather he stated that the Sabbath was to help man, not man to help the Sabbath.

> And He said to them, "The Sabbath was made for man, and not man for the Sabbath (Mark 2:27).

Several other translations help to see the real meaning of Jesus' statement...

"IS IT OKAY TO PRAY IN TONGUES IN CHURCH?"

3 And He said to the man who had the withered hand, "Step forward."

4 Then He said to them, "Is it lawful on the Sabbath to do good or to do evil, to save life or to kill?" But they kept silent.

5 And when He had looked around at them with anger, being grieved by the hardness of their hearts, He said to the man, "Stretch out your hand." And he stretched it out, and his hand was restored as whole as the other (Mark 3:1-5).

Jesus never compromised the promises of God in the fear of someone being offended. On the Sabbath He healed people, set the captives free, made the blind to see, and even called the Pharisees whitewashed tombs for denying the power of God to operate (Matthew 23:27).

4 Jesus answered and said to them, "Go and tell John the things which you hear and see:

5 The blind see and the lame walk; the lepers are cleansed and the deaf hear; the dead are raised up and the poor have the gospel preached to them.

6 And blessed is he *who is not offended* because of Me" (Matthew 11:4-6).

12 Then His disciples came and said to Him, "Do You know that *the Pharisees were offended* when they heard this saying?"

13 But He answered and said, "Every plant which My heavenly Father has not planted will be uprooted.

5 Then Philip went down to the city of Samaria and preached Christ to them.

6 And the multitudes with one accord heeded the things spoken by Philip, hearing and seeing the miracles which he did.

7 For unclean spirits, crying with a loud voice, came out of many who were possessed; and many who were paralyzed and lame were healed.

8 And there was great joy in that city (Acts 8:4-8).

Paul encourages the church to operate in the power of God rather than in the wisdom of men!

For I am not ashamed of the gospel of Christ, for it is the *power of God* to salvation for everyone who believes, for the Jew first and also for the Greek (Romans 1:16).

For the message of the cross is foolishness to those who are perishing, but to us who are being saved it is the *power of God* (1 Corinthians 1:18).

4 And my speech and my preaching were not with persuasive words of human wisdom, but in *demonstration of the Spirit and of power*,

5 that your faith should not be in the wisdom of men but in the *power of God* (1 Corinthians 2:4-5).

But what about the possibility of offending someone and they leave the church never to return? I would question and say; did Jesus ever water down his message? Did

"IS IT OKAY TO PRAY IN TONGUES IN CHURCH?"

he ever *not* heal anyone or do miracles in the temple so they would not be offended? Look at one of His discourses...

> 33 But whoever denies Me before men, him I will also deny before My Father who is in heaven.
>
> 34 "Do not think that I came to bring peace on earth. I did not come to bring peace but a sword.
>
> 35 For I have come to 'set a man against his father, a daughter against her mother, and a daughter-in-law against her mother-in-law';
>
> 36 and 'a man's enemies will be those of his own household.'
>
> 37 He who loves father or mother more than Me is not worthy of Me. And he who loves son or daughter more than Me is not worthy of Me.
>
> 38 And he who does not take his cross and follow after Me is not worthy of Me.
>
> 39 He who finds his life will lose it, and he who loses his life for My sake will find it (Matthew 10:33-39).

These may seem like very harsh statements, but they are the truth. Jesus did not let man run the Sabbath services; rather he stated that the Sabbath was to help man, not man to help the Sabbath.

> And He said to them, "The Sabbath was made for man, and not man for the Sabbath (Mark 2:27).

Several other translations help to see the real meaning of Jesus' statement...

> 27 Jesus finished by saying, "People were not made for the good of the Sabbath. The Sabbath was made *for the good of people.*
> 28 So the Son of Man is Lord over the Sabbath" (Mark 2:27-28 CEV).

> 27 Then Jesus said to them, "The Sabbath was made *to meet the needs of people,* and not people to meet the requirements of the Sabbath.
> 28 So the Son of Man is Lord, even over the Sabbath!" (Mark 2:27-28 NLT).

> 27 But the Sabbath was *made to benefit man,* and not man to benefit the Sabbath.
> 28 And I, the Messiah, have authority even to decide what men can do on Sabbath days!" (Mark 2:27-28 The Living Bible).

It's very obvious what the Lord has decided we can do on the Sabbath, by what he did for the woman with the issue of blood, and the man with the withered hand…

> So ought not this woman, being a daughter of Abraham, whom Satan has bound—think of it—for eighteen years, *be loosed from this bond on the Sabbath?"* (Luke 13:16).

> 1 And He entered the synagogue again, and a man was there who had a withered hand.
> 2 So they watched Him closely, whether He would heal him on the Sabbath, so that they might accuse Him.

"IS IT OKAY TO PRAY IN TONGUES IN CHURCH?"

3 And He said to the man who had the withered hand, "Step forward."

4 Then He said to them, "Is it lawful on the Sabbath to do good or to do evil, to save life or to kill?" But they kept silent.

5 And when He had looked around at them with anger, being grieved by the hardness of their hearts, He said to the man, "Stretch out your hand." And he stretched it out, and his hand was restored as whole as the other (Mark 3:1-5).

Jesus never compromised the promises of God in the fear of someone being offended. On the Sabbath He healed people, set the captives free, made the blind to see, and even called the Pharisees whitewashed tombs for denying the power of God to operate (Matthew 23:27).

4 Jesus answered and said to them, "Go and tell John the things which you hear and see:

5 The blind see and the lame walk; the lepers are cleansed and the deaf hear; the dead are raised up and the poor have the gospel preached to them.

6 And blessed is he *who is not offended* because of Me" (Matthew 11:4-6).

12 Then His disciples came and said to Him, "Do You know that *the Pharisees were offended* when they heard this saying?"

13 But He answered and said, "Every plant which My heavenly Father has not planted will be uprooted.

14 Let them alone. They are blind leaders of the blind. And if the blind leads the blind, both will fall into a ditch" (Matthew 15:12-14).

The Pharisaic Spirit

The Pharisaic spirit is a spirit which advocates strict religious rituals and ceremonies to accomplish forgiveness and righteousness in the sight of God. The definition pertains to the Pharisees and is defined as "practicing or advocating strict observance of external forms and ceremonies of religion or conduct without regard to the spirit; self-righteous; hypocritical."[2] It's a spirit of righteousness through works instead of faith in Christ. It's a denial that salvation is by faith. It's a denial that healing is available for sinners. It's a denial that the Gifts of the Spirit are for unbelievers. It's a stifling of the power of God due to unbelief in the righteousness that Christ attained for us on the Cross even while we were yet sinners (Romans 5:8).

The Pharisees did not accept the healing and deliverance through Jesus as the works of God, because it was not being done through them! They were self-righteous. They were losing control of the people. Their livelihood (income) was at stake. They were snakes and vipers!

---

[2] Pharisaic. (n.d.). Dictionary.com Unabridged (v 1.1). Retrieved June 16, 2007, from Dictionary.com website: http://dictionary.reference.com/browse/pharisaic

13 "But woe to you, scribes and Pharisees, hypocrites! For you shut up the kingdom of heaven against men; for you neither go in yourselves, nor do you allow those who are entering to go in.

14 Woe to you, scribes and Pharisees, hypocrites! For you devour widows' houses, and for a pretense make long prayers. Therefore you will receive greater condemnation.

15 "Woe to you, scribes and Pharisees, hypocrites! For you travel land and sea to win one proselyte, and when he is won, you make him twice as much a son of hell as yourselves (Matthew 23:13-15).

23 "Woe to you, scribes and Pharisees, hypocrites! For you pay tithe of mint and anise and cummin, and have neglected the weightier matters of the law: justice and mercy and faith. These you ought to have done, without leaving the others undone.

24 Blind guides, who strain out a gnat and swallow a camel!

25 "Woe to you, scribes and Pharisees, hypocrites! For you cleanse the outside of the cup and dish, but inside they are full of extortion and self-indulgence.

26 Blind Pharisee, first cleanse the inside of the cup and dish, that the outside of them may be clean also.

27 "Woe to you, scribes and Pharisees, hypocrites! For you are like whitewashed tombs which indeed appear beautiful outwardly, but inside are full of dead men's bones and all uncleanness.

28 Even so you also outwardly appear righteous to men, but inside you are full of hypocrisy and lawlessness (Matthew 23:23-28).

Serpents, brood of vipers! How can you escape the condemnation of hell? (Matthew 23:33).

So back to the question; is it ok to pray in tongues in church? Paul said in 1 Corinthians 14:18-19; "I thank my God I speak with tongues more than you all; yet in the church I would rather speak five words with my understanding, that I may teach others also, than ten thousand words in a tongue."

This has caused much misunderstanding within the church. If Paul's words are true in 1 Corinthians chapter 2, that our faith needs to stand in the power of God instead of the wisdom of men, we need to take that into consideration as we analyze chapter 14.

CHAPTER THREE

Establishing Important Key Truths

The First Key Truth

There is a difference between the operation of our personal prayer language and the operation of the nine Gifts of the Spirit mentioned in 1 Corinthians 12:4-11.

The chart following shows that the nine Gifts of the Spirit can be divided into three general categories, the Inspiration Gifts, the Revelation Gifts, and the Power Gifts. All the gifts are from the Holy Spirit, so we could say that there is one Holy Spirit, three categories, nine gifts with the three gifts in each category. The three gifts that Paul is specifically writing about in chapter fourteen are the three inspiration gifts that say something; Different Kinds of Tongues, Interpretation of Tongues, and Prophecy.

"IS IT OKAY TO PRAY IN TONGUES IN CHURCH?"

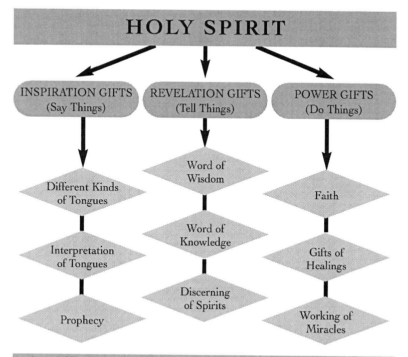

One Holy Spirit / Three categories / Nine gifts / Three gifts in each category

The difference between the operation of the nine gifts and the operation of our personal prayer language is:

A) The 9 Gifts of the Spirit operate only *"as He wills"*... The word of wisdom, word of knowledge, gift of faith, gifts of healings, working of miracles, gift of prophecy, discerning of spirits, different kinds of tongues, and interpretation of tongues.

But one and the same Spirit works all these things, distributing to each one individually *as He wills* (1 Corinthians 12:11).

B) Our personal prayer language operates *"as I will,"*…

What is the conclusion then? *I will* pray with the spirit, and *I will* also pray with the understanding. *I will* sing with the spirit, and *I will* also sing with the understanding (1 Corinthians 14:15).

This means we *cannot* operate in the nine gifts at any time by our own will, however, we *CAN* pray or sing in our own personal prayer language at any time by our will for the purpose we choose. In chapter sixteen we will discuss ten good reasons to pray in tongues.

The Second Key Truth

When we are speaking in our "understood language"; (that would be English for me), either through the Gifts of the Spirit as *"He wills"* — OR — in our own prayer language as *"we will"*, we are speaking to both *God AND man*. However, when we are speaking in other tongues, either through the Gifts of the Spirit as *"He wills"* — OR — in our own prayer language as *"we will"*, we are speaking to *God and not man!*

> 2 For he who speaks in a tongue *does not speak to men but to God*, for no one understands him; however, in the spirit he speaks mysteries.
> 3 But he who prophesies *speaks edification and exhortation and comfort to men.*

"IS IT OKAY TO PRAY IN TONGUES IN CHURCH?"

4 He who speaks in a tongue edifies himself, but he who prophesies edifies the church (1 Corinthians 14:2-4).

It's obvious that if we speak in a known or understood language both God and man can understand us. It's also obvious that when we speak in other tongues we are not speaking to man, because Paul said no one understood him. Paul even said in verse 14 that when He spoke in other tongues he himself did not understand what he was saying!

But what about Acts chapter two when they spoke in other tongues and the people heard them in their own languages? This brings us to a third truth...

The Third Key Truth

Speaking in Tongues can operate in both the understood languages of men and the languages of Angels that cannot be understood by man.

Though I speak with the tongues of men and of angels, but have not love, I have become sounding brass or a clanging cymbal (1 Corinthians 13:1).

This brings us to the main purpose of Paul's teaching in chapters 12-14: whatever we do, it must all be done in love. This is something that we will cover more fully in chapter eleven.

The Fourth Key Truth

The two gifts of the Spirit, "Speaking in Tongues" and "Interpretation of Tongues", when operated together equal the gift of Prophecy.

The gift of the Spirit "Speaking in Tongues" can be defined as "a supernatural utterance in an <u>unknown</u> tongue." The definition of "Interpretation of Tongues," can be defined as "the supernatural interpretation of that which was spoken in an <u>unknown</u> tongue." The Gift of Prophecy can be defined as "a supernatural utterance in a <u>known</u> tongue." Prophecy does not need interpretation. When the gift of Speaking in Tongues has been interpreted, it is now equal to prophecy—a supernatural utterance in a <u>known</u> tongue.

Why then does God use tongues? One reason He created them was to be a sign to the unbeliever and uninformed (1 Corinthians 14:22). If He was concerned about offending them, He would not have made them a Gift of the Spirit!

CHAPTER FOUR

It Depends on Who You Are Speaking To!

18 I thank my God I speak with tongues more than you all;

19 yet in the church I would rather speak five words with my understanding, that I may teach others also, than ten thousand words in a tongue (1 Corinthians 14:18-19).

To answer the question: "Is it ok to pray in tongues in a church service?" I have found the following answer to help unwind the seemingly confusing statements Paul makes in 1 Corinthians 14.

The answer is simply… "It depends on who are you speaking to!"

"IS IT OKAY TO PRAY IN TONGUES IN CHURCH?"

I'll say it in one sentence to make it clear... Is it ok to pray in tongues in a church service? Well, it depends on who you are speaking to!

Let's Study Chapter 14 Verse by Verse

> Pursue love, and desire spiritual gifts, but especially that you may prophesy (1 Corinthians 14:1).

Paul states in this verse we should desire the spiritual gifts, they should operate in love toward others, but we should especially desire to prophesy. Why? Because prophecy is always something understood by the person it is being spoken to. If you are speaking to someone, it will only benefit them if they understand what you are saying! Remember key fact #4 though; the operation of Tongues and Interpretation of Tongues together equal prophecy, because it is understood by the hearer.

There is another definition of prophecy that is also important to know at this point.

> And I fell at his feet to worship him. But he said to me, "See that you do not do that! I am your fellow servant, and of your brethren who have the testimony of Jesus. Worship God! *"For the testimony of Jesus is the spirit of prophecy"* (Revelation 19:10).

This means that as we witness, testify, share, teach, or preach the gospel of Jesus Christ, it is the spirit of

It Depends on Who You Are Speaking To!

prophecy. Why? Because these are all spoken in a known language and understood by the hearer. Paul is saying that one of the best things we should desire in spiritual gifts, "when we are speaking to people," is that they understand what we are saying!

> For he who speaks in a tongue does not speak to men but to God, for no one understands him; however, in the spirit *he speaks mysteries* (1 Corinthians 14:2).

It depends on who you are speaking to! If we are speaking in tongues to God, man does not necessarily have to understand it.

Mysteries

In the spirit you are speaking "mysteries" (1 Corinthians 14:2). As was mentioned in the introduction, the definition of the original Greek word "mysteries" is "that which, being outside the range of unassisted natural apprehension, can be made known only by divine revelation, and is made known in a manner and at a time appointed by God, and to those only who are illumined by His Spirit."[3] This means that it is not up to us whether we

---

[3] Vine, W., Unger, M. F., & White, W. (1997, c1996). *Vine's complete expository dictionary of Old and New Testament words* (electronic ed.) (2:424). Nashville: Thomas Nelson.

"IS IT OKAY TO PRAY IN TONGUES IN CHURCH?"

understand it or not. It is up to God whether it is interpreted or not. Obviously, He will only give us the interpretation if He wants us to have it.

> For one who speaks in an [unknown] tongue speaks not to men but to God, for no one understands or catches his meaning, because in the [Holy] Spirit he utters secret truths and hidden things [not obvious to the understanding] (1 Corinthians 14:2 AMP).

> But if your gift is that of being able to "speak in tongues," that is, to speak in languages you haven't learned, you will be talking to God but not to others, since they won't be able to understand you. You will be speaking by the power of the Spirit, but it will all be a secret (1 Corinthians 14:2 The Living Bible).

> If you praise him in the private language of tongues, God understands you but no one else does, for you are sharing intimacies just between you and him (1 Corinthians 14:2 The Message).

However, if we are speaking through prophecy to man, it is always understood by the hearer and should be edifying, exhorting, and comforting.

> But he who prophesies speaks edification and exhortation and comfort to men (1 Corinthians 14:3).

This verse is very helpful information! Know this: that prophecy through (1) the Gift of the Spirit—Prophecy, (2) the Gifts of the Spirit—Tongues, and Interpretation of

It Depends on Who You Are Speaking To!

Tongues operating together, or (3) the testimony of Jesus (preaching, teaching, witnessing and testifying), should always bring edification, exhortation, and comfort to the hearer. Therefore, if you hear a message in a service that is supposed to be from God, but it is condemning, degrading, and depressing, do not accept it as a prophetic word!

> He who speaks in a tongue edifies himself, but he who prophesies edifies the church (1 Corinthians 14:4).

Since it depends on who you are speaking to, then if you are speaking to God in tongues and you do not know what is being said, it does not need to be interpreted. Amazingly, this process will still edify the one doing the speaking! Why? Well, to answer this question we need to go to the book of Jude.

> But you, beloved, building yourselves up on your most holy faith, praying in the Holy Spirit (Jude 20).

To pray in the Holy Spirit, is both praying in a known language led by the Spirit and it is also praying in other tongues. Jude 20 says that as we pray in tongues we will build up (or edify) ourselves in our faith. Why?

It's the same as needing *muscles* to lift weights.

Since it takes *muscles* to lift weights…

Then as we continue to lift the weights it "builds up" our *muscles*.

"IS IT OKAY TO PRAY IN TONGUES IN CHURCH?"

In the same way, you need *faith* to pray in tongues.

Since it takes *faith* to pray in tongues…

Then as we continue to pray in tongues, it "builds up" our *faith*.

Notice that this does not give us faith, but it builds up the faith we already have. The only way for faith to come is by hearing, and hearing by the Word of God (Romans 10:17). Once you get faith from the Word, then you can edify and build your faith stronger by praying in the spirit.

So who gets edified? The one who speaks in tongues to God! However, when you speak to the church, it takes prophecy for the church to be edified. Why? Because it must be understood. So if you are speaking to the church, prophesy and they will be edified. Again, that's (1) the Gift of the Spirit—Prophecy, (2) The Gifts of the Spirit—Tongues, and Interpretation of Tongues operating together, or (3) the testimony of Jesus (preaching, teaching, witnessing and testifying).

> I wish you all spoke with tongues, but even more that you prophesied; for he who prophesies is greater than he who speaks with tongues, unless indeed he interprets, that the church may receive edification (1 Corinthians 14:5).

He wants us all to speak with tongues and talk to God. But when you speak to the church (people) we

It Depends on Who You Are Speaking To!

should prophesy and not just speak in tongues so they may be edified. This verse also proves that the Gift of Tongues with Interpretation of Tongues is equal to Prophecy because it says "unless indeed he interprets." Paul continues...

> But now, brethren, if I come to you speaking with tongues, what shall I profit you unless I speak to you either by revelation, by knowledge, by prophesying, or by teaching? (1 Corinthians 14:6).

Again, this agrees with Revelation 19:10b "... For the testimony of Jesus is the spirit of prophecy." To speak by revelation or knowledge would be preaching, teaching, and prophesying, all in the understanding, not in tongues, unless they are interpreted.

> 7 Even things without life, whether flute or harp, when they make a sound, unless they make a distinction in the sounds, how will it be known what is piped or played?
> 8 For if the trumpet makes an uncertain sound, who will prepare for battle?
> 9 So likewise you, unless you utter by the tongue words easy to understand, how will it be known what is spoken? For you will be speaking into the air (1 Corinthians 14:7-9).

If you are speaking to the people in the church, do it in the understanding! Paul shows us by using inanimate objects as musical instruments, they can be understood as

"IS IT OKAY TO PRAY IN TONGUES IN CHURCH?"

long as they make distinctive sounds. A trumpet's melody, if understood, can assemble an army for battle; however, if the sound is not distinctive it will produce no results. Likewise, this is how we should operate our church assembly so it will be profitable for those who attend.

> 10 There are, it may be, so many kinds of languages in the world, and none of them is without significance.
>
> 11 Therefore, if I do not know the meaning of the language, I shall be a foreigner to him who speaks, and he who speaks will be a foreigner to me.
>
> 12 Even so you, since you are zealous for spiritual gifts, let it be for the edification of the church that you seek to excel (1 Corinthians 14:10-12).

Yes, Paul is encouraging us to be zealous for the gifts to operate; however, let's make sure that when they do operate, they edify the church. He is instructing us to keep the vision and purpose of the Gifts. This purpose is to benefit the body of Christ as a whole.

In verse 14 Paul speaks of the differences between speaking (praying) in tongues ourselves to God, and speaking in a known language to man...

> Therefore let him who speaks in a tongue pray that he may interpret (1 Corinthians 14:13).

When we speak in tongues by our own will to God in our prayer language of tongues—pray that we **MAY** interpret. Interpretation is not required because we are speaking to God. However, as God wills (and we ask for it) He will give us the interpretation if it will benefit us.

Romans 8:26-27 says that when we are praying in the spirit, we are praying for saints according to the will of God. Sometimes the interpretation might help us, and other times it may not be any of our business. We might not even know the people we are praying for. We are actually praying the prayer requests of Jesus, the one who always intercedes for the world.

> Therefore He is also able to save to the uttermost those who come to God through Him, *since He always lives to make intercession for them* (Hebrews 7:25).
>
> For if I pray in a tongue, my spirit prays, but my understanding is unfruitful (1 Corinthians 14:14).

This is helpful information. The Word of God is the only thing that can divide between soul (mind) and spirit (heart). Hebrews 4:12 says, "For the word of God is living and powerful, and sharper than any two-edged sword, piercing even to the division of soul and spirit, and of joints and marrow, and is a discerner of the thoughts and intents of the heart." Paul clearly states that when we pray in tongues, it is our spirit praying not our understanding (mind). This is why we do not understand what we are praying. It is a supernatural spirit-to-Spirit language between our spirit and the Spirit of God. Do not be

"IS IT OKAY TO PRAY IN TONGUES IN CHURCH?"

concerned if you do not understand what you are saying. Paul did not understand it either!

> 15 What is the conclusion then? I will pray with the spirit, and I will also pray with the understanding. I will sing with the spirit, and I will also sing with the understanding.
>
> 16 Otherwise, if you bless with the spirit, how will he who occupies the place of the uninformed say "Amen" at your giving of thanks, since he does not understand what you say?
>
> 17 For you indeed give thanks well, but the other is not edified (1 Corinthians 14:15-17).

It depends on who you are speaking (or singing) to! If you are speaking to man, speak in a known language, and if you are speaking to God, speak in tongues, and pray you may interpret. There are two ways to pray. Both are excellent and necessary. If you know what to pray, pray in your known language and understanding. If you do not know what to pray, pray in tongues. When there are others around you that need to hear and understand what it is that you are praying, pray in a language they understand.

> 18 I thank my God I speak with tongues more than you all;
>
> 19 yet in the church I would rather speak five words with my understanding, that I may teach others also, than ten thousand words in a tongue (1 Corinthians 14:18-19).

It Depends on Who You Are Speaking To!

In a church service there are people—at least there should be! If we want the people to be edified WE SHOULD RATHER use a language that will be understood. I WOULD RATHER does not mean "I don't speak in tongues," but it is Paul's preference to be understood. It all depends on who you are speaking to. If you are in church and you are speaking to God, then you can use a known and unknown language (tongues). But if you are speaking to people, then speak in the understanding.

What we need to understand in the time that Paul was writing, church services were getting out of hand. They were too tilted toward <u>just</u> praying in tongues. No effort was made to edify the people by revelation or knowledge, teaching or prophecy. This is what Paul was attempting to correct. People were leaving church services without being edified because there was no prophecy through the Word being taught or by the Gifts of the Spirit. The services were too spiritual to be any earthly good!

Paul did not say "don't pray in tongues." He said he was thankful he prayed in tongues more than they did; however, he clarified his statement by saying if the choice was one or the other—he would RATHER prophecy! But it would be much better to have both! Verse 39 proves this because he says "do not forbid to speak with tongues."

Therefore, brethren, desire earnestly to prophesy, and *do not forbid* to speak with tongues (1 Corinthians 14:39).

"IS IT OKAY TO PRAY IN TONGUES IN CHURCH?"

Here are verses 15-19 with a few additions (my additions to help clarify)…

15 What is the conclusion then? I will pray with the spirit (*when I am speaking to God*), and I will also pray with the understanding (*when I am speaking to man*). I will sing with the spirit (*when I am singing to God*), and I will also sing with the understanding (*when I am singing to man*).

16 Otherwise, if you bless with the spirit, how will he who occupies the place of the uninformed say "Amen" at your giving of thanks, since he does not understand what you say?

17 For you indeed give thanks well (*to God*), but the other (*man*) is not edified.

18 I thank my God I speak with tongues more than you all;

19 yet in the church *I would rather* speak five words with my understanding, that I may teach others also, than ten thousand words in a tongue (1 Corinthians 14:15-19).

Is it okay to pray in tongues in church? Someone might interpret verses 18-19 to say no, but in verse 39 Paul definitely says yes! The reason for this is that it depends on who you are speaking to! Obviously, if you preach or teach in tongues no one will learn anything!

Notice that verse 18 gives us another use of our prayer language of tongues—"to give thanks well." While you wouldn't want to thank a person in other tongues, you *can* give thanks well to God, and there is nothing wrong to pray or worship God in other tongues corporately since we are talking to Him.

What about the prayer of agreement? Can it be prayed corporately in other tongues?

> Again I say to you that if two of you agree on earth concerning anything that they ask, it will be done for them by My Father in heaven (Matthew 18:19).

Yes, it is ok to pray in tongues in a church service, depending on who you are speaking to, however, what about the prayer of agreement? How can believers corporately pray together and "agree" if they do not know what is being said?

In a church group of believers if we understand and "agree" that praying in tongues is praying the perfect will of God according to Romans 8:26-27, and that we are giving thanks well according to 1 Corinthians 14:17, shouldn't we be able to pray corporately in tongues, agree and say AMEN?

> 26 Likewise the Spirit also helps in our weaknesses. For we do not know what we should pray for as we ought, but the Spirit Himself makes intercession for us with groanings which cannot be uttered.
> 27 Now He who searches the hearts knows what the mind of the Spirit is, because He makes intercession for the saints *according to the will of God* (Romans 8:26-27).

"IS IT OKAY TO PRAY IN TONGUES IN CHURCH?"

Can we pray and agree corporately in other tongues? Yes, we can agree in a corporate prayer meeting as we pray in other tongues, because we know and believe that we are praying according to the perfect will of God. We can all say "Amen." If you can't agree with the will of God, then I would never recommend you pray in tongues personally or corporately! Can this apply to singing in the Spirit also? Yes, as we worship together and give God thanks by singing to Him in other tongues, we can all be in unity and agreement.

CHAPTER FIVE

Why Did God Invent Tongues?

20 Brethren, do not be children in understanding; however, in malice be babes, but in understanding be mature.

21 In the law it is written: "With men of other tongues and other lips I will speak to this people; And yet, for all that, they will not hear Me," says the Lord (1 Corinthians 14:20-21).

Paul is quoting the prophetic word from Isaiah…

11 For with stammering lips and another tongue He will speak to this people,

12 To whom He said, "This is the rest with which You may cause the weary to rest," And, "This is the refreshing"; Yet they would not hear (Isaiah 28:11-12).

"IS IT OKAY TO PRAY IN TONGUES IN CHURCH?"

Everything that God has done or is doing in the New Testament was prophesied in the Old Testament. Why? Because this is how God creates.

> 22 So Jesus answered and said to them, "Have faith in God.
>
> 23 For assuredly, I say to you, whoever *says* to this mountain, 'Be removed and be cast into the sea,' and does not doubt in his heart, but believes that those things he *says* will be done, he will have whatever he *says*.
>
> 24 Therefore I say to you, whatever things you ask when you pray, believe that you receive them, and you will have them (Mark 11:22-24).

The 'God kind of faith' creates by believing in your heart and confessing with your mouth. This is how God Himself created the world. Then God said, "let there be light," and there was light (Genesis 1:3). Then God said, "let there be firmament" (Genesis 1:6). Then God said, "let the waters" (Genesis 1:9). Then God said, "let the earth" (Genesis 1:11). Then God said, "let there be lights... (Genesis 1:14). Then God said, let us make man in our own image (Genesis 1:26).

This is why God had to confuse the "one-language" of the whole earth at the Tower of Babel. The people were one; they believed in their hearts and confessed with their mouth that they would build a tower whose top is the heavens. God knew if He did not stop this that they would accomplish their goal. It was not His will, nor would it be a good thing for the people, so He confused their language which broke the unity, their faith, and the work immediately ceased.

> 1 Now the whole earth had one language and one speech.
>
> 2 And it came to pass, as they journeyed from the east, that they found a plain in the land of Shinar, and they dwelt there.
>
> 3 Then they said to one another, "Come, let us make bricks and bake them thoroughly." They had brick for stone, and they had asphalt for mortar.
>
> 4 And they said, "Come, let us build ourselves a city, and a tower whose top is in the heavens; let us make a name for ourselves, lest we be scattered abroad over the face of the whole earth."
>
> 5 But the Lord came down to see the city and the tower which the sons of men had built.
>
> 6 And the Lord said, "Indeed the people are one and they all have one language, and this is what they begin to do; now nothing that they propose to do will be withheld from them.
>
> 7 Come, let Us go down and there confuse their language, that they may not understand one another's speech."
>
> 8 So the Lord scattered them abroad from there over the face of all the earth, and they ceased building the city.
>
> 9 Therefore its name is called Babel, because there the Lord confused the language of all the earth; and from there the Lord scattered them abroad over the face of all the earth (Genesis 11:1-9).

Could the gift of tongues be the Tower of Babel restored? Could tongues be the "one-world" language restored; however, this time in the perfect will of God? The Hebrew word "babel" means confusion.[4] The Tower of Babel was God's confusion of language. The Greek word for "tongues" in Acts 2:4 is "glossa" meaning "the language or dialect used by a particular people distinct from that of other nations."[5] As God's people and "nation" could praying in other or "new" tongues be His whole earth—one nation's "heavenly" language?

Jesus is always interceding on our behalf (Hebrews 7:25), but if God has truly given us free will, then He cannot go against our will even though Jesus has prayed. Jesus has His own prayer list for us, but if we are not in agreement and we do not speak them out into the earth's atmosphere—"prophesy them," then they cannot come to pass. How can we pray the perfect will of God if we don't know the will of God and we see through a glass darkly (1 Corinthians 13:12)?

---

[4] Strong, J. (1996). *The exhaustive concordance of the Bible : Showing every word of the test of the common English version of the canonical books, and every occurrence of each word in regular order.* (electronic ed.) (H894). Ontario: Woodside Bible Fellowship.

[5] Strong, J. (1996). *The exhaustive concordance of the Bible: Showing every word of the test of the common English version of the canonical books, and every occurrence of each word in regular order.* (electronic ed.) (G1100). Ontario: Woodside Bible Fellowship.

This is the reason God created the language of other (or new) tongues. When we do not know His perfect will, or we are "confused" as to how to proceed or what to speak, we can pray in other tongues and prophesy His will for us and others. Can you imagine the power of God's people (His entire nation) speaking "one-language," believing with our hearts, and confessing with our mouths the perfect will of God? THERE IS NOTHING THAT THEY PURPOSE TO DO THAT WILL BE WITHHELD FROM THEM (Genesis 11:6)!

If this is true (and it is), then the language of other tongues is as much canon as the Word of God itself! "Tongues are just as much canonized as the Word of God! They are as powerful in the spirit realm as the declaration of written scriptures." Dr. Douglas Wingate[6]

To answer the question "why did God invent the language of other (or new) tongues," the answer is simply "to have His will prayed and prophesied on the earth, giving Him permission to accomplish His will for the saints."

---

[6] Wingate, Douglas, Dr. *The Anointing*, Romans 8:26-27, Life Christian University 2000.

CHAPTER SIX

Tongues— A "Sign" to Unbelievers— Not the Message

22 Therefore tongues are for a sign, not to those who believe but to unbelievers; but prophesying is not for unbelievers but for those who believe.

23 Therefore if the whole church comes together in one place, and all speak with tongues, and there come in those who are uninformed or unbelievers, will they not say that you are out of your mind?

24 But if all prophesy, and an unbeliever or an uninformed person comes in, he is convinced by all, he is convicted by all.

25 And thus the secrets of his heart are revealed; and so, falling down on his face, he will worship God and report that God is truly among you (1 Corinthians 14:22-25).

"IS IT OKAY TO PRAY IN TONGUES IN CHURCH?"

Is it okay to pray in tongues in church? What if there is an unbeliever or uninformed person in the service? What we must understand is that tongues are *"a sign"* for the unbeliever—they are not *"the message"* for the unbeliever!

Remember, "these *signs* will follow those who believe" (Mark 16:17-18). Who will the signs follow? Will it only follow believers and those who are informed? Let's take a look at the five signs and how they operated:

1) **Cast out demons:** Should we not cast out demons from the uninformed and unbelievers? Jesus cast out demons from unbelievers all the time!

   When evening had come, they brought to Him many who were demon-possessed. And He cast out the spirits with a word, and healed all who were sick (Matthew 8:16).

   But if I cast out demons with the finger of God, surely the kingdom of God has come upon you (Luke 11:20).

Should not the Kingdom of God come upon the uninformed and unbelievers!

2) **Take up serpents:** If you study this carefully you will understand this is *not* referring to "handling snakes," but rather taking spiritual authority over the devil. Should we not take authority over the devil among unbelievers! The Bible very clearly

declares that Satan is "that old serpent" (Revelation 20:2). Jesus took authority over the devil in front of unbelievers all the time. Even if it is a real poisonous snake, right in front of unbelievers, when Paul was accidentally bitten by a poisonous snake (and I say accidentally—he was handling wood not a snake), he took his authority by faith, shook the snake into the fire, and did not die (Acts 28:3-6)!

3) **If they drink anything deadly it will by no means hurt them:** Does this mean we should get some strychnine poison and test this out? No! The key word here is "if." If—meaning by accident or unknown cause. This is why we should always pray according to the Word before we eat or drink.

> 4 For every creature of God is good, and nothing is to be refused if it is received with thanksgiving;
>
> 5 for it is sanctified by the word of God and prayer (1 Timothy 4:4-5).

Should we not believe to live and not die in front of unbelievers! Should we not pray over our food in front of those who are uninformed! Yes, we should! We are to be examples of the power of God in our lives to everyone who is around us. We are to keep our candles lit so the whole world can see our faith. Don't hide what you believe—cast out demons and take authority over Satan!

"IS IT OKAY TO PRAY IN TONGUES IN CHURCH?"

Wherever you live, there are many things that can cause you harm or even death. Spiders, snakes, ticks, scorpions, mosquitoes, poisonous bugs, frogs, fish, bad water, spoiled food, viruses, germs, bacteria's, heavy weather, earthquakes, tragic accidents, and evil people who kill and maim. Thank God we can pray for His protection: to live and not die, to be healthy and not sick!

4) **Lay hands on the sick and they will recover:** Should we not lay hands on sick unbelievers! Jesus laid hands on sick unbelievers all the time and they were healed! Talk about a sign!

> When the sun was setting, all those who had any that were sick with various diseases brought them to Him; and He laid His hands on every one of them and healed them (Luke 4:40).

5) **They shall speak with new tongues:** Should this fifth sign be handled differently than the other four! Can it *only* be done in front of those who believe and are informed!

All five signs are for the uninformed and the unbeliever! Paul clarifies this when he says "they (speaking in tongues) are a sign—to unbelievers" (1 Corinthians 14:22). If it never happens in front of unbelievers or the uninformed, then they will not see the sign! What are signs? Signs are designed to head you in the right direction! Mark 16:17 says these SIGNS will follow those who believe. This word "signs" is from the original Greek word "semeion" meaning "a mark, a token, an unusual occurrence transcending the common course of nature."[7] Vine's Complete Expository Dictionary of Old and New Testament Words states it "is used of 'miracles' and wonders as signs of divine authority."[8]

I remember one Sunday morning this young couple, Joshua and Susan, came to our church for the first time. They met a member of our church, Chad, in a local store. Because this couple was wearing Christian t-shirts and jewelry, Chad introduced himself and invited them to come to a service. They came and due to their hunger and love for the Lord, they walked right up front and sat in the front row! This is unusual for visitors.

After worship, the Spirit of God began to move in the Gifts, and there were a few prophecies, tongues and interpretation, and we even prayed together as a congregation in the Spirit without any interpretation (as we spoke to God and not man). I did not know it, but Joshua was very offended. He wanted desperately to stand up and leave the

---

[7] Strong, J. (1996). *The exhaustive concordance of the Bible : Showing every word of the test of the common English version of the canonical books, and every occurrence of each word in regular order.* (electronic ed.) (G4592). Ontario: Woodside Bible Fellowship.

[8] Vine, W. E., Unger, M. F., & White, W. (1996). *Vine's complete expository dictionary of Old and New Testament words* (2:412). Nashville: T. Nelson.

"IS IT OKAY TO PRAY IN TONGUES IN CHURCH?"

service, but for some reason he could not do it—something held him in his seat.

Amazingly enough, although they did not know why, the next week they returned and sat in the same seats! Following the service, they came and spoke to me and wanted to take my wife and me to dinner. The Lord told me that they wanted to inquire about the Holy Spirit and tongues, so I came prepared with material I had written on the subject. We had a great dinner and discussion. After dinner we went out to their car in the parking lot and they both prayed, received the baptism of the Holy Spirit, and spoke in tongues! Since then, they have joined the church and became leaders in the youth ministry! Thank God we did not squelch the move of the Spirit of God in our church service!

Is this is how everyone will react? No, some will be offended and if they do not leave during the service, they certainly will not return next week. Jesus never took a stance to please everyone. On the contrary, He obeyed God, and many left because his message was too strong for them!

60 Therefore many of His disciples, when they heard this, said, "This is a hard saying; who can understand it?"
61 When Jesus knew in Himself that His disciples complained about this, He said to them, *"Does this offend you?*

62 What then if you should see the Son of Man ascend where He was before?

63 *It is the Spirit who gives life; the flesh profits nothing. The words that I speak to you are spirit, and they are life.*

64 But there are some of you who do not believe." For Jesus knew from the beginning who they were who did not believe, and who would betray Him.

65 And He said, "Therefore I have said to you that no one can come to Me unless it has been granted to him by My Father."

66 *From that time many of His disciples went back and walked with Him no more* (John 6:60-66).

It is the Spirit who gives life! Remember, "These signs will follow those who believe" (Mark 16:15). I am a believer; I pray you are too!

It's interesting how the word translated "uninformed" in the New King James Version is the original Greek word *"idiotes."*[9]

This is where we get the English word idiot. The King James Version translates it unlearned, the Amplified says ungifted and uninitiated, Darby says simple persons, the Contemporary English Version says outsiders, the Good News Translation—ordinary people, the International

---

[9] Strong, J. (1996). *The exhaustive concordance of the Bible: Showing every word of the text of the common English version of the canonical books, and every occurrence of each word in regular order.* (electronic ed.) (G2399). Ontario: Woodside Bible Fellowship.

"IS IT OKAY TO PRAY IN TONGUES IN CHURCH?"

Standard Version—uneducated people, the New American Bible—uninstructed, and the New Living Translation—people who do not understand. What we need to realize is that tongues are a sign (a miracle and wonder) for the *simple, uneducated, unlearned, uninstructed, ordinary, uninitiated, unbelieving outsiders who do not understand!*

Is it okay to pray in tongues in church? I am so glad we did!

CHAPTER SEVEN

The Fifth Key is "All"

22 Therefore tongues are for a sign, not to those who believe but to unbelievers; but prophesying is not for unbelievers but for those who believe.

23 Therefore if the whole church comes together in one place, and **ALL** speak with tongues, and there come in those who are uninformed or unbelievers, will they not say that you are out of your mind?

24 But if **ALL** prophesy, and an unbeliever or an uninformed person comes in, he is convinced by all, he is convicted by **ALL**.

25 And thus the secrets of his heart are revealed; and so, falling down on his face, he will worship God and report that God is truly among you (1 Corinthians 14:22-25).

The key is *ALL*—if that is *ALL* you do, they will think you are mad.

"IS IT OKAY TO PRAY IN TONGUES IN CHURCH?"

However, if prophesy comes in a known language, it becomes a message they can understand. Somebody has to preach, teach, and minister in a known language!

Two interesting definitions of the Greek word in this verse for "all" is "everything" and "all the time."[10] If we do everything in tongues, and continually speak in tongues the whole time without speaking in a known language, we are not acting in love, we are not edifying anybody, (other than ourselves) and they will think we are mad!

Generally, unless it's a dedicated prayer meeting, I believe a spirit-filled church service should be 90—95% in a known language so that all understand and are edified.

Is it okay to pray in tongues in church?

It is definitely okay to have the Gifts of the Spirit— Tongues, Interpretation of Tongues, and Prophecy—but it is also okay to pray in tongues together as a congregation, as long as that is **NOT ALL WE DO,** because not everybody will be edified!

Why is prophesying not for unbelievers but for those who believe (verse 22)? It's actually very simple if you think it through. Unbelievers do not naturally understand

---

[10] Strong, J. (1996). *The exhaustive concordance of the Bible: Showing every word of the text of the common English version of the canonical books, and every occurrence of each word in regular order.* (electronic ed.) (G3956). Ontario: Woodside Bible Fellowship.

The Fifth Key is "All"

and believe in the Gifts of the Spirit. Therefore, when they hear the "sign" of tongues it naturally gains their attention and interest. When they hear the interpretation, they are convicted and the secrets of their hearts are revealed. Believers are just that—they already believe—they do not need tongues to get their attention—they do not need the "sign." Therefore, they easily can recognize and receive the Gifts of the Spirit by faith. They are already tuned in spiritually and can recognize a "word from the Lord." They can easily hear what the Spirit is saying through prophecy in any form it comes in.

CHAPTER EIGHT

Can We Only Have Two or Three?

26 How is it then, brethren? Whenever you come together, each of you has a psalm, has a teaching, has a tongue, has a revelation, has an interpretation. Let all things be done for edification.

27 If anyone speaks in a tongue, let there be two or at the most three, each in turn, and let one interpret.

28 But if there is no interpreter, let him keep silent in church, and let him speak to himself and to God.

29 Let two or three prophets speak, and let the others judge.

30 But if anything is revealed to another who sits by, let the first keep silent.

31 For you can all prophesy one by one, that all may learn and all may be encouraged.

"IS IT OKAY TO PRAY IN TONGUES IN CHURCH?"

32 And the spirits of the prophets are subject to the prophets.

33 For God is not the author of confusion but of peace, as in all the churches of the saints (1 Corinthians 14:26-33).

There is much dispute about verse 27. Many believe that Paul is stating that there can be at the most three, "gift of tongues" in a service. Paul is speaking about the "Gifts of the Spirit" and not our personal prayer language. If we balance verse 27 with three of our previous key truths from chapter three, it will help us understand Paul's instruction.

Key One: The nine Gifts of the Spirit are as "He wills," and our personal prayer language of tongues is as "we will."

Key Two: The Gifts of the Spirit are God speaking to us; our personal prayer language of tongues is us speaking to God.

Key Four: The two Gifts of the Spirit "Speaking in Other Tongues" and "Interpretation of Tongues" operating together, equal the "Gift of Prophecy" in a known tongue.

Is Paul really stating that in a church service there should be at the most two or three prophetic words from God? No, if you read it correctly, he is saying that the Gift of Tongues should not operate more than two or three times without then the Gift of Interpretation. Once it is

Can We Only Have Two or Three?

interpreted, you can allow two or three more Gifts of the Spirit; however, again, it should be interpreted before another Gift of Tongues takes place. If there is no interpreter, then the Gift should not operate. Why is this? Because if it is a "Gift of the Spirit" (God speaking to us), then we need to understand what it is He wants us to know. It might be a Word of Knowledge or Word of Wisdom. We should not let the Gift of Tongues operate more than two or three times without the Gift of Interpretation, so the people may receive edification.

To further explain this process, Paul states in verse 29 that ALL can prophesy, one by one, that all may learn and all be encouraged. Then he tells us that we should judge the prophecy to be sure it is actually a word from God and not something someone just made up. We should always compare the tongues, interpretation, and prophecy with the Word of God. Does the word given line up with scripture? If not, count it a false prophecy. Does it speak edification, exhortation, and comfort to men? Paul states that this is what prophecy is supposed to do in verse three. If you hear doom, gloom, unscriptural statements or instructions, do not accept it as a word from God!

No! You should not have more than two or three bring forth the Gift of Tongues until the Gift of Interpretation takes place. Yes! Once there has been interpretation, you can follow the process again, again, and again as the Spirit

"IS IT OKAY TO PRAY IN TONGUES IN CHURCH?"

of God wills. Each time, we should judge the word. If there is no interpreter, the Gift of Tongues should not operate because no one will be edified. Verse 33 sums it up by saying that God is not the author of confusion. In other words, the operation of the Gifts, are to bless and benefit God's people, not to confuse anyone. This lines up with verse 40 which says "Let all things be done decently and in order."

CHAPTER NINE:

Can Women Prophesy?

34 Let your women keep silent in the churches, for they are not permitted to speak; but they are to be submissive, as the law also says.

35 And if they want to learn something, let them ask their own husbands at home; for it is shameful for women to speak in church.

36 Or did the word of God come originally from you? Or was it you only that it reached?

37 If anyone thinks himself to be a prophet or spiritual, let him acknowledge that the things which I write to you are the commandments of the Lord.

38 But if anyone is ignorant, let him be ignorant (1 Corinthians 14:34-38).

The King James Version puts verse 36 this way: "What? came the word of God out from

"IS IT OKAY TO PRAY IN TONGUES IN CHURCH?"

you? or came it unto you only?"

What is Paul trying to say? While it is true that the Old Testament law says "...Your desire shall be for your husband, and he shall rule over you" (Genesis 3:16), the New Testament says, "There is neither Jew nor Greek, there is neither slave nor free, *there is neither male nor female; for you are all one in Christ Jesus*" (Galatians 3:28).

When we take into consideration the prophecy of Joel that Peter read in Acts 2:18 "And on *My menservants and on My maidservants* I will pour out My Spirit in those days; And they shall prophesy," and when we read about Philip the evangelists daughters in Acts 21:9, "Now this man had four virgin daughters who prophesied," we can understand the statement, "WHAT? came the word of God out from you? or came it unto you only?" Paul was rebuking them for their misunderstanding of the Word, and instructing them to allow the gifts to flow through women as Joel prophesied it would. He ended his statement on this issue by saying let the ignorant be ignorant! Therefore, in verse 39, he says "do not forbid to speak with tongues."

I like the way Wuest New Testament says it, "So that, my brethren, be desiring earnestly to be imparting to others divine revelations, and stop forbidding the speaking in tongues. But let all things be done in a seemly manner and in a right order" (1 Corinthians 14:39-40 WUESTNT).

CHAPTER TEN:

The Sixth Key is "All Things"

39 Therefore, brethren, desire earnestly to prophesy, and do not forbid to speak with tongues.

40 Let **all things** be done decently and in order (1 Corinthians 14:39-40).

Let how many things?—*LET ALL THINGS!*

What "things" are we speaking about? We are speaking about the operation of two things during a church service, the Gifts of the Spirit as "He wills," and our personal prayer language as "we will."

Nowhere in 1 Corinthians does Paul tell the church *not* to pray or sing in tongues. He does, however, tell the church how to operate in the nine gifts of the Spirit and in praying and singing in other tongues. Paul is instructing

"IS IT OKAY TO PRAY IN TONGUES IN CHURCH?"

the church to have a balance between the Spirit world and the natural world.

In 14:4-5 he doesn't say not to speak in tongues, only that interpretation is better, and in the following verses he explains why. Again in verse 19—if he had to choose between the two, He would *rather* prophesy in a known tongue or have the two gifts, Tongues and Interpretation of Tongues, operate together that all may receive edification. In verse 20, he tells us to be mature in our understanding and in verse 21, he quotes Isaiah 28:11-12, which says that He (God) will speak to men using other tongues and they will not hear Him. This again explains the next verse which declares that tongues are a sign for unbelievers.

CHAPTER ELEVEN

The Seventh Key is Love

Though I speak with the tongues of men and of angels, but have not love, I have become sounding brass or a clanging cymbal (1 Corinthians 13:1).

It's interesting how chapter 12 is about gifts, both the Gifts of the Spirit and the gifts given men such as apostles, teachers, helps, governments, etc. Chapter 14 is about the operation of these gifts in the church and chapter 13, in the middle of chapters 12 and 14, is all about love.

Paul teaches that no matter how great the gifts of God or man may be, they must all be operated in the spirit of love toward others.

The Living Bible translation puts it very clearly;

4 Love is very patient and kind, never jealous or envious, never boastful or proud,

"IS IT OKAY TO PRAY IN TONGUES IN CHURCH?"

5 never haughty or selfish or rude. Love does not demand its own way. It is not irritable or touchy. It does not hold grudges and will hardly even notice when others do it wrong.

6 It is never glad about injustice, but rejoices whenever truth wins out.

7 If you love someone, you will be loyal to him no matter what the cost. You will always believe in him, always expect the best of him, and always stand your ground in defending him (1 Corinthians 13:4-7 The Living Bible).

None of the gifts should be used to abuse people, gain control of them, or prophesy money out of their pockets! This is a common practice that we see often when a minister prophesies that if people give a certain amount of money in the offering, they will receive a special prosperity anointing or an angel will appear to them within a week. These are false prophets! The only one they want to prosper is themselves!

The gifts should not be used to lift oneself in pride as if we are someone great having the "Word of the Lord." The Gifts should not be faked. Faking the Gifts could lead people to believe we are a great prophet. No! The gifts are to edify, exhort, and comfort, as stated in chapter 14, verse 3. Our use of the Gifts of God and of man should be for the benefit of others! As we desire the spiritual gifts, we should also pursue love (1 Corinthians 14:1). This is why Paul stated that we need to judge the prophets (1 Corinthians 14:29) to determine whether they are true or false. Anything outside of love, whether tongues of men or angels, faith that can move mountains, or knowledge of all mysteries, is worth nothing—nothing at all.

The manifestation of the Spirit is given for the profit of all...

> To each is given the manifestation of the Spirit *for the common good* (1 Corinthians 12:7 ESV).
>
> The Holy Spirit displays God's power through each of us as a means of *helping the entire church* (1 Corinthians 12:7 The Living Bible).

Our liberty should be used to love and serve others, not to bring glory to ourselves.

> For you, brethren, have been called to liberty; only do not use liberty as an opportunity for the flesh, *but through love serve one another* (Galatians 5:13).

CHAPTER TWELVE

New Testament Prayer Meetings

1 When the Day of Pentecost had fully come, they were all with one accord in one place.

2 And suddenly there came a sound from heaven, as of a rushing mighty wind, and it filled the whole house where they were sitting.

3 Then there appeared to them divided tongues, as of fire, and one sat upon each of them.

4 And they were all filled with the Holy Spirit and began to speak with other tongues, as the Spirit gave them utterance (Acts 2:1-4).

This came about from the prophecy written from the Prophet Joel…

14 But Peter, standing up with the eleven, raised his voice and said to them, "Men of Judea and all who

"IS IT OKAY TO PRAY IN TONGUES IN CHURCH?"

dwell in Jerusalem, let this be known to you, and heed my words.

15 For these are not drunk, as you suppose, since it is only the third hour of the day.

16 But this is what was spoken by the prophet Joel:

17 'And it shall come to pass in the last days, says God, That I will pour out of My Spirit on all flesh; Your sons and your daughters shall prophesy, Your young men shall see visions, Your old men shall dream dreams.

18 And on My menservants and on My maidservants I will pour out My Spirit in those days; And they shall prophesy.

19 I will show wonders in heaven above And signs in the earth beneath: Blood and fire and vapor of smoke.

20 The sun shall be turned into darkness, And the moon into blood, Before the coming of the great and awesome day of the LORD.

21 And it shall come to pass That whoever calls on the name of the LORD Shall be saved' (Acts 2:14-21).

The argument could be that they *only* spoke the languages of man. Verse 5 states there were men from every nation under heaven. They were confused because they heard this group of 120 disciples speak in their own foreign language. They were amazed and could not understand how these men and women (Mary, Jesus' mother included), could be speaking in the language from their country: Parthians, Medes, Elamites, those who lived in Mesopotamia, Judea, Cappadocia, Pontus, Asia, Phrygia,

Pamphylia, Egypt, the part of Libya that joins Cyrene, Rome, Cretans, and Arabs. If I am reading this correctly, they heard the wonderful works of God being spoken in 15 different known (understood) languages. However, some accused them of being drunk. Why? *Obviously, because there were some of the 120 who spoke in languages no one understood.* Some were speaking in the understood languages of man and others were speaking in the non-understood languages of angels (1 Corinthians 13:1). Peter's message beginning in verse 14 was addressed particularly to those who did not understand the language for he says; "These are not drunk as you suppose," and then he quotes the prophet Joel from Joel chapter two.

This was God's doing and it all happened in the presence of unbelievers! I see this as proof that "tongues are a sign for the unbeliever." If God did not want the unbelievers to see or hear it, He wouldn't have allowed it publicly. Remember, this was something He did, not man.

Do we really think they *did not* pray in tongues in Acts Chapter Four?

> And when they had prayed, the place where they were assembled together was shaken; and they were all **filled with the Holy Spirit,** and they spoke the word of God with boldness (Acts 4:31).

Do we really think they *did not* pray in tongues in Acts Chapter Six?

"IS IT OKAY TO PRAY IN TONGUES IN CHURCH?"

3 Therefore, brethren, seek out from among you seven men of good reputation, **full of the Holy Spirit** and wisdom, whom we may appoint over this business;

4 but we will give ourselves **continually to prayer** and to the ministry of the word."

5 And the saying pleased the whole multitude. And they chose Stephen, a man **full of faith and the Holy Spirit,** and Philip, Prochorus, Nicanor, Timon, Parmenas, and Nicolas, a proselyte from Antioch,

6 whom they set before the apostles; and **when they had prayed,** they laid hands on them (Acts 6:3-6).

Do we really think they *did not* pray in tongues in Acts Chapter 8?

14 Now when the apostles who were at Jerusalem heard that Samaria had received the word of God, they sent Peter and John to them,

15 who, when they had come down, **prayed for them that they might receive the Holy Spirit.**

16 For as yet He had fallen upon none of them. They had only been baptized in the name of the Lord Jesus.

17 Then they laid hands on them, and **they received the Holy Spirit.**

18 And when Simon saw that through the laying on of the apostles' hands the Holy Spirit was given, he offered them money (Acts 8:14-18).

What did Simon see? They were already saved but had not yet received the Baptism of the Holy Spirit, and after

Peter and John laid hands on them they received the Holy Spirit. How did Simon know that this group received the Holy Spirit? The answer is that he must have seen (and heard) them speak in other tongues.

A good question…

If we are not to pray in tongues as a group in a congregational setting, *how then can a group of people receive the Holy Spirit in a congregational or public meeting?* Would this not be an excellent definition of "tongues are a sign for unbelievers?" Simon was recently saved but was totally unfamiliar with the Baptism of the Holy Spirit! He was uninformed as 1 Corinthians 14:23-24 says. But when he "saw" it manifested in a public meeting he was not offended. He wanted it so much he was willing to pay for it! How would this have ever happened if they did not allow praying in tongues in a public corporate meeting?

The Holy Spirit falls in the home of Cornelius!

44 While Peter was still speaking these words, the Holy Spirit fell upon all those who heard the word.

45 And those of the circumcision who believed were astonished, as many as came with Peter, because the gift of the Holy Spirit had been poured out on the Gentiles also.

46 For they heard them speak with tongues and magnify God. Then Peter answered,

"IS IT OKAY TO PRAY IN TONGUES IN CHURCH?"

47 "Can anyone forbid water, that these should not be baptized who have received the Holy Spirit just as we have?" (Acts 10:44-47).

This passage shows us several important things. One: salvation does not include the Baptism of the Holy Spirit, it is an additional gift for those who are already saved if they will receive it by faith. Two: hearing them speak in other tongues was the proof that the gift of the Holy Spirit was poured out and received. Three: the gift is for gentile believers also. Four: baptism in water is not how to obtain salvation. This is evident in this passage because they were already saved, filled with the Holy Spirit, and spoke in tongues before they were baptized in water.

Another prayer meeting...

5 Peter was therefore kept in prison, but *constant prayer* was offered to God for him by the church.
12 So, when he had considered this, he came to the house of Mary, the mother of John whose surname was Mark, where many were gathered together praying (Acts 12:5 & 12).

What were they praying? Obviously they were praying for Peter; however, it's most likely that they did not pray specifically that an angel would hand carry him out of prison. Is it possible that they prayed in tongues in this prayer gathering? The Bible does not define specifically how they prayed, but as spirit-filled believers I believe they spoke both in the understanding and in the Spirit. This way they were praying the perfect will of God, and it brought about a miracle!

As they ministered to the Lord... the Holy Spirit said...

1 Now in the church that was at Antioch there were certain prophets and teachers: Barnabas, Simeon who was called Niger, Lucius of Cyrene, Manaen who had been brought up with Herod the tetrarch, and Saul.

2 **As they ministered to the Lord and fasted, the Holy Spirit said,** "Now separate to Me Barnabas and Saul for the work to which I have called them."

3 Then, having fasted and prayed, and laid hands on them, they sent them away (Acts 13:1-3).

Again, there is no mention of tongues in this passage, but we must consider two terms that are written here: "as they ministered to the Lord" and "The Holy Spirit said." Paul remarks in 1 Corinthians 14, that we can speak to God and not to man, speak in the language of angels, pray, sing, and give thanks well to Him in other tongues. Combine this with Acts chapter two, where they magnified God and then in Acts ten, where they ministered to the Lord, to conclude that they did not pray in tongues would be wrong. These were spirit-filled believers who prayed both in the understanding and the Spirit.

"IS IT OKAY TO PRAY IN TONGUES IN CHURCH?"

It's clear they prayed in tongues in Acts Chapter 19!

1 And it happened, while Apollos was at Corinth, that Paul, having passed through the upper regions, came to Ephesus. And finding some disciples

2 he said to them, "Did you receive the Holy Spirit when you believed?" So they said to him, "We have not so much as heard whether there is a Holy Spirit."

3 And he said to them, "Into what then were you baptized?" So they said, "Into John's baptism."

4 Then Paul said, "John indeed baptized with a baptism of repentance, saying to the people that they should believe on Him who would come after him, that is, on Christ Jesus."

5 When they heard this, they were baptized in the name of the Lord Jesus.

6 And when Paul had laid hands on them, the Holy Spirit came upon them, and they spoke with tongues and prophesied.

Now the men were about twelve in all (Acts 19:1-7).

This is another passage that proves that the Baptism of the Holy Spirit does not come automatically with salvation, for Paul asked "did you receive the Holy Spirit when you believed?" Their answer was "we have not so much as heard whether there is a Holy Spirit." This group of disciples were already saved but had not yet received the Baptism of the Holy Spirit! Paul shared the Word to them more clearly and they received the gift, spoke in tongues and prophesied.

CHAPTER THIRTEEN

What About "Tongues Shall Cease"?

Love never fails. But whether there are prophecies, they will fail; whether there are tongues, they will cease; whether there is knowledge, it will vanish away (1 Corinthians 13:8).

There is a very simple solution to this verse that many people have misunderstood. If we take the three things mentioned, prophecies, tongues, and knowledge, and determine their purpose, we can then determine when they will fail, cease, and vanish. We need to do this, in context, realizing that all three will change at the same time.

Have all prophecies yet ended? No! There are still prophecies to be fulfilled. There are many end-time prophecies mentioned in Daniel and Revelation that are

"IS IT OKAY TO PRAY IN TONGUES IN CHURCH?"

still to take place. After they have been fulfilled, all biblical prophecies will have ended.

What about knowledge? Has it ended? No! We are still learning; however, there is coming a time when we will *all* "know Him" as stated in Jeremiah.

> No more shall every man teach his neighbor, and every man his brother, saying, 'Know the Lord,' for they all shall know Me, from the least of them to the greatest of them, says the Lord. For I will forgive their iniquity, and their sin I will remember no more (Jeremiah 31:34).

When the Great White Throne judgment takes place, even the unsaved will have the full knowledge of who He is and bow before Him.

> For it is written: "As I live, says the Lord, Every knee shall bow to Me, And every tongue shall confess to God" (Romans 14:11).

As we can see, both prophecies and knowledge (in the sense of knowing God) will come to an end in the last of the last days before eternity begins.

If we take these two in context, then the third, tongues, will cease at the same time—at the end of time. This makes sense because at that time we will not need to know what to pray for as we ought (Romans 8:26-27). The Gifts of the

Spirit will not be necessary to assist mankind. Miracles and Gifts of Healings will all be complete.

> 9 For we know in part and we prophesy in part.
>
> 10 But when that which is perfect has come, then that which is in part will be done away (1 Corinthians 13:9-10).

When will everything be perfect? When we are all spending eternity in Heaven!

> For now we see in a mirror, dimly, but then face to face. Now I know in part, but then I shall know just as I also am known (1 Corinthians 13:12).

Now, we are limited by our humanness—we have not yet been perfected. We still have a corruptible and unregenerate flesh, mind, and body. We will not need tongues in Heaven because we will know Him as He knows us; therefore, at that time tongues, prophecies, and the unknown knowledge of Him will cease.

It's very evident what we need now is prophecy to be fulfilled, tongues to pray when we do not know what to pray, knowledge to assist us in our walk with Him, and to lead others to Him. We need all three until the day we spend eternity with Him in Heaven!

CHAPTER FOURTEEN

How to Be Saved

In the Gospel of John chapter three, Jesus talked to Nicodemus about the new birth. He said unless one is "born again" he cannot see the Kingdom of God. Nicodemus had trouble understanding this, so Jesus made it clearer. He said unless one is born of water and of the Spirit, he cannot enter the Kingdom of God. Born of water is our natural birth (from the mother's womb) and born of the Spirit is becoming a child of God. The words "born again" mean born from above. It's accepting God by faith as your Heavenly Father. You may have heard other words for it: being saved, becoming a new creature in Christ, asking Jesus in your heart, making Jesus the Lord of your life, etc.

It's a simple two step process as mentioned in the book of Romans…

"IS IT OKAY TO PRAY IN TONGUES IN CHURCH?"

9 that if you confess with your mouth the Lord Jesus and believe in your heart that God has raised Him from the dead, you will be saved.

10 For with the heart one believes unto righteousness, and with the mouth confession is made unto salvation (Romans 10:9-10).

Verse 9—confess with your mouth and believe in your heart

Verse 10—believe with your heart and confess with your mouth

Why a two step process? Because believing is not enough! Even Satan himself BELIEVES that Jesus is the Son of God. He believes that Jesus died on the cross for the sins of the world. He believes that Jesus rose from the dead and is seated at the right hand of God in heaven. You could say that Satan is a strong believer! If anyone believes, he does! However, even though he believes that Jesus is the Savior, he has never confessed with his mouth that Jesus is his Lord. He hates Jesus. He has never asked him to forgive his sins. He has never asked Jesus to be the Lord of his life. He has never asked Jesus to come into his heart! He never has, and according to scripture, he never will.

For "whoever calls on the name of the Lord shall be saved" (Romans 10:13).

Satan has never called upon the name of the Lord to be saved! He has never done step two. Are you any different than Satan! Do you believe in your heart but have never called upon Jesus to be your Lord! Have you ever asked Him to forgive you of your sins! Are you born from above! If not, like Satan, you will not see or enter the Kingdom of Heaven!

GOD'S WORD IS CLEAR!

- If you confess with your mouth, and believe with your heart—YOU WILL BE SAVED! (verse 9)
- If you believe with your heart, and confess with your mouth—YOU WILL RECEIVE SALVATION! (verse 10)
- If you call upon the Lord—YOU SHALL BE SAVED! (verse 13)

If you are a believer, but have never called upon the Name of the Lord to be saved, let's do it right now!

To Receive Jesus as Your Lord, Pray This Prayer

"Lord Jesus, I believe in my heart that you are the Son of God, you died on the cross for my sins, and you rose from the dead. I ask you to forgive me of my sins and to cleanse me from all unrighteousness. I call on you now and

"IS IT OKAY TO PRAY IN TONGUES IN CHURCH?"

ask you to come into my heart and become my Lord and Savior. Thank you for forgiving me and giving me eternal life. With my mouth, I now confess you as my Savior and Lord! Amen!"

CHAPTER FIFTEEN

Now is the Time— Be Baptized in the Holy Spirit!

And they were all filled with the Holy Spirit and began to speak with other tongues, as the Spirit gave them utterance (Acts 2:4).

Six Steps to be Baptized in the Holy Spirit and Speak with other tongues!

1. You must first be saved!

   He said to them, "Did you receive the Holy Spirit when you believed?" So they said to him, "We have not so much as heard whether there is a Holy Spirit" (Acts 19:2).

"IS IT OKAY TO PRAY IN TONGUES IN CHURCH?"

2. If you ask for the Holy Spirit, He will fill you!

   If you then, being evil, know how to give good gifts to your children, how much more will your heavenly Father give the Holy Spirit to those who ask Him!" (Luke 11:13).

3. You will do the praying!

   I thank my God I speak with tongues more than you all (1 Corinthians 14:18).

4. You will not understand what you are praying!

   For if I pray in a tongue, my spirit prays, but my understanding is unfruitful (1 Corinthians 14:14).

5. You are speaking to God!

   For he who speaks in a tongue does not speak to men but to God, for no one understands him; however, in the spirit he speaks mysteries (1 Corinthians 14:2).

6. You are praying God's will!

   26 Likewise the Spirit also helps in our weaknesses. For we do not know what we should pray for as we ought, but the Spirit Himself makes intercession for us with groanings which cannot be uttered.

   27 Now He who searches the hearts knows what the mind of the Spirit is, because He makes intercession for the saints according to the will of God (Romans 8:26-27).

Now is the Time—Be Baptized in the Holy Spirit!

THE OPERATION OF PRAYING IN TONGUES

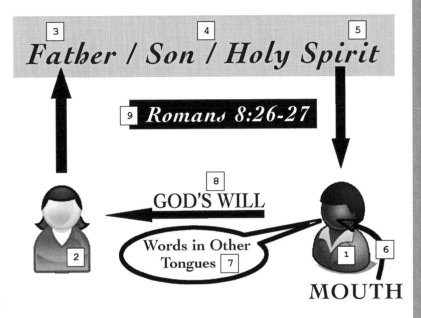

Follow the Numbers!

Peter (1) wants to pray for Mary (2), but he doesn't know what she needs. The only one who knows exactly what she needs is the Father, "God" (3), the Son, "Jesus" (4), and the Holy Spirit (5). The Holy Spirit wants to pray for Mary, but He doesn't have a mouth on the Earth to pray. Peter has a mouth (6). If Peter will receive the Baptism of the Holy Spirit and pray in tongues (7), then the Holy Spirit can take the words he speaks in other tongues and pray God's will for Mary (8). The Scripture that explains this is Romans 8:26-27 (9). This type of prayer is very powerful because it's always, without fail, the perfect will of God!

The New Living Translation puts it in very simple terms...

> 26 And the Holy Spirit helps us in our weakness. For example, we don't know what God wants us to pray for. But the Holy Spirit prays for us with groanings that cannot be expressed in words.
>
> 27 And the Father who knows all hearts knows what the Spirit is saying, for the Spirit pleads for us believers in harmony with God's own will (Romans 8:26-27 NLT).

How I Received the Baptism of the Holy Spirit

When I was a young teenager, I was at an auto show with my family and a friend in New York City. My friend and I were hungry, so, we left the convention center to go next door to a sandwich vending shop. As we walked through the halls, took the escalator, walked the sidewalk and entered the shop, we heard several people talking in foreign languages, and we decided we would pretend we were from another country too! We made up a language and talked to each other as if we understood what we were saying. I would say something like *"hablah jume torakami"*, and he would laugh and respond with something just as meaningless. We did it all the way to and from the store. I am not sure if anyone knew it was all made up gibberish.

Now is the Time—Be Baptized in the Holy Spirit!

Fast forwarding to 1979... I was saved February 11th when I was just one month shy of 26 years old. Within a year after being saved, I heard the Word taught concerning the Baptism of the Holy Spirit several times, and I was reading a book by Ralph M. Riggs titled "The Spirit Himself."[11] When I reached chapter thirteen "The Baptism in the Holy Spirit, How to Receive It," I knew it was time for me to receive. The five sub-titles within the chapter were, "let us now receive, we must first be saved, we must obey, we must ask, we must believe,"—I was ready!

Sitting there alone reading at my desk in my apartment, I prayed and asked the Lord to fill me with His Holy Spirit, and then by faith I began to speak in other tongues. I decided to pray for the President of the United States, and since I did not know what to pray for as I ought, I prayed for him in other tongues. After a minute or so, Satan spoke to my mind and told me that I was making it up. He said it was nothing but baby talk and it didn't mean a thing. I immediately opened my Bible to Romans 8:26-27 and told him that I was not making it up, it was not baby talk, and that according to Romans I was praying the will of God for the president. I continued to pray in other tongues and Satan came a second time with the same accusation—"you are making it up, it is just a bunch of baby

---

[11] Riggs, Ralph M. *The Spirit Himself*. Springfield Missouri: Gospel Publishing House, 1949

"IS IT OKAY TO PRAY IN TONGUES IN CHURCH?"

talk." I rebuked him, repeated what the book of Romans said and prayed in tongues even louder. Satan came a third time, but this time he said something that shook me. He said "then what's the difference between what you are doing now, and what you did at the auto show with your friend in New York City?" It stopped me. I did not have the answer. I sat there. Then I brought the question to the Lord. I said "Lord, what is the difference between what I am doing now and what I did as a teenager in New York?" Almost instantly, the Lord spoke. He gave me one word—FAITH! He said "it's according to your faith. The signs follow those who believe. If you believe, then you are praying My will. If you don't, it amounts to nothing." That's all I needed, and I have been praying in tongues ever since! Satan did not return with his accusation a fourth time! It's been 27 years since then, and I pray more in tongues now than I ever have. Praying in Tongues is the most practical and useful tool the Lord has ever given me.

What proof do we have that we are actually praying God's Will? The only proof we have is His Word and our faith! Like a quote I heard Kenneth E. Hagin say "The Bible says it, I believe it, and that settles it!"

Now is the Time—Be Baptized in the Holy Spirit!

A Song God Gave Me to Teach Children

Power[12]

Power, yes Power
Power from on High
Holy Spirit, His Power
Power from on High

On the day of Pentecost believers got a gift
Tongues of fire sat on them from Heaven up above
Jesus sent the Power it was Power from on High
This was the coming day of which Joel had prophesied

Jesus said go nowhere till you're filled with the promise
Baptized in the Holy Ghost so you become a witness
Why did He say wait and do nothing till it came?
It's cause the Power makes the Gift's work in His Name!

In obedience to Jesus I asked for the gift
Luke 11:13 told me if I'd ask He'd give
And then by faith I started to pray in other tongues
The Word was true it came I got it, and it was fun!

The devil came and told me it was baby talk
I showed him scripture out of Romans chapter 8
I said no I was praying in God's will for saints
These signs will follow those who believe and walk in faith

---

[12] Langlois, James Kennedy. *Power*, Captain Charismatic, Icongo, ASCAP, 1998

"IS IT OKAY TO PRAY IN TONGUES IN CHURCH?"

Yes it is practical……… you can use it to pray in God's will
Yes it is wonderful…… it will edify your spirit man
Yes it is spiritual……… you're speaking to God and not to man
Yes it is powerful……… it takes all the limits off your prayers
These signs will follow those
Who believe in my Name they will
Cast out demons they will speak with new tongues
They will take up serpents, if they

Drink anything deadly it will
Not hurt them, they will lay hands
On the sick, and they will recover
Oh yes they will, His Word is true!

Paul called it tongues of Angels
Speaking to God and not to man
In the Spirit speaking mysteries
God's secrets of the Heavenlies

He who speaks in an unknown tongue edifies himself
Paul thanked God he spoke in tongues more than all of us
He told the Ephesians to use it to tear down the strongholds of the devil
He told the Corinthians to pray *and* sing in the Spirit

I asked the Lord "What's the difference between baby talk and tongues?"
He gave me just one mighty word….

"Faith" He said, "It's the key that makes it happen, and it's the only way to receive and walk in this gift"
Is there any other proof that Tongues are real?
No, the only proof we have is the Word!
What about "Tongues, they shall cease"?
Yes! When we get to Heaven at the end of Satan's lease
We won't need them anymore because he'll be in the Eternal Lake of Fire!
How do I receive the Power?
Read Luke 11 verses 9 through 13
If you ask, He'll give it to you!
Acts 2:39 says "The Promise is to *YOU!*"

To Receive the Baptism of the Holy Spirit and Speak With New Tongues, Pray This Prayer

"Lord Jesus, I ask you to baptize me in the Holy Spirit with the evidence of speaking in new tongues. You said if I asked for the Holy Spirit, you would fill me. I thank you for filling me with your Spirit! Now by faith I will pray in new tongues! I realize I will not understand what I am saying, but I believe what the Bible says in 1 Corinthians chapter 14 and Romans chapter 8. I believe I am speaking to you and I believe I am praying *your will!* Amen!"

Now! Go ahead and think of someone to pray for and pray for them in other tongues!

CHAPTER SIXTEEN

Ten Good Reasons to Pray in Tongues

1. To pray when you don't know what to pray.

    Likewise the Spirit also helps in our weaknesses. For we do not know what we should pray for as we ought, but the Spirit Himself makes intercession for us with groanings which cannot be uttered (Romans 8:26).

2. To pray God's will when you don't know God's will.

    Now He who searches the hearts knows what the mind of the Spirit is, because He makes intercession for the saints according to the will of God (Romans 8:27).

"IS IT OKAY TO PRAY IN TONGUES IN CHURCH?"

3. To speak to God and not to man.

   For he who speaks in a tongue does not speak to men but to God, for no one understands him; however, in the spirit he speaks mysteries (1 Corinthians 14:2).

4. To speak the language of Angels.

   Though I speak with the tongues of men and of angels, but have not love, I have become sounding brass or a clanging cymbal (1 Corinthians 13:1).

5. To pray with the Spirit.

   What is the conclusion then? I will pray with the spirit, and I will also pray with the understanding (1 Corinthians 14:15a).

6. To sing with the Spirit.

   I will sing with the spirit, and I will also sing with the understanding (1 Corinthians 14:15b).

7. To magnify God.

   For they heard them speak with tongues and magnify God. Then Peter answered, (Acts 10:46).

8. To give thanks well.

   For you indeed give thanks well, but the other is not edified (1 Corinthians 14:17).

9. To stay filled with the Spirit.

   And do not be drunk with wine, in which is dissipation; but be filled with the Spirit,

   speaking to one another in psalms and hymns and spiritual songs, singing and making melody in your heart to the Lord, (Ephesians 5:18-19).

10. To edify (build up) yourself on your faith.

    He who speaks in a tongue edifies himself, but he who prophesies edifies the church (1 Corinthians 14:4).

    But you, beloved, building yourselves up on your most holy faith, praying in the Holy Spirit, (Jude 20).

CHAPTER SEVENTEEN

Developing Your Prayer Language

Many times I see those who receive the Baptism of the Holy Spirit and pray in tongues for the first time somewhat disappointed by their limited words and flow with their new heavenly language. They have heard tongues spoken by others in a very articulate and expressive way. Some only receive a syllable or two and wonder if it's really new tongues. Have no fear! Welcome to the crowd! A new language takes time to develop. Just like a baby learns new words every day, as God's children, we will acquire new words and expressions as we pray in other tongues every day.

I suggest praying in tongues while driving in the car. It's a great place that does not disturb others. You can

"IS IT OKAY TO PRAY IN TONGUES IN CHURCH?"

practice and let the Lord give you more words and expressions. After a while you will have just as expressive a language as others do. Any place you can be alone is a great place to develop your new prayer language. I suggest attending spirit-filled prayer meetings. Let your faith do the walking and your spirit do the talking! You now have an unlimited prayer life. You have no boundaries or weaknesses: you can pray at any time. If you know what to pray you can pray in the understanding; if you do not know what to pray, you can pray in other tongues. You now have the confidence that you are praying according to the perfect will of God! Luke calls it "power from on high" (Luke 24:49).

CHAPTER EIGHTEEN

How to Stay Filled With the Spirit

1. *Speak and sing to yourself* in psalms, hymns, and spiritual songs

   17 Therefore do not be unwise, but understand what the will of the Lord is.

   18 And do not be drunk with wine, in which is dissipation; but *be filled with the Spirit,*

   19 *speaking to one another in psalms and hymns and spiritual songs,* singing and making melody in your heart to the Lord,

   20 giving thanks always for all things to God the Father in the name of our Lord Jesus Christ, (Ephesians 5:17-20).

   Spiritual songs can be sung both with the understanding and with the spirit (other tongues). As

"IS IT OKAY TO PRAY IN TONGUES IN CHURCH?"

Paul said in 1 Corinthians 14:15, he would sing both ways.

What is the conclusion then? I will pray with the spirit, and I will also pray with the understanding. I will sing with the spirit, and I will also sing with the understanding (1 Corinthians 14:15).

2. *Speak and sing to one another* in psalms, hymns, and spiritual songs.

   Let the word of Christ dwell in you richly in all wisdom, teaching and *admonishing one another in psalms and hymns and spiritual songs*, singing with grace in your hearts to the Lord (Colossians 3:16).

3. *Give* thanks always for all things unto God

   And whatever you do in word or deed, do all in the name of the Lord Jesus, giving thanks to God the Father through Him (Colossians 3:17).

4. *Build* yourself up by praying in the Holy Sprit

   But you, beloved, building yourselves up on your most holy faith, praying in the Holy Spirit, (Jude 20)

5. *Hear* the Word

   So then faith comes by hearing, and hearing by the word of God (Romans 10:17).

6. *Confess* the Word

   Let no corrupt word proceed out of your mouth, but what is good for necessary edification, that it may impart grace to the hearers (Ephesians 4:29).

   8 But what does it say? "The word is near you, in your mouth and in your heart" (that is, the word of faith which we preach):

   9 that if you confess with your mouth the Lord Jesus and believe in your heart that God has raised Him from the dead, you will be saved.

   10 For with the heart one believes unto righteousness, and with the mouth confession is made unto salvation (Romans 10:8-10).

CHAPTER NINETEEN

Declaration of Independence

1 And I, brethren, when I came to you, did not come with excellence of speech or of wisdom declaring to you the testimony of God.

2 For I determined not to know anything among you except Jesus Christ and Him crucified.

3 I was with you in weakness, in fear, and in much trembling.

4 *And my speech and my preaching were not with persuasive words of human wisdom, but in demonstration of the Spirit and of power,*

5 *that your faith should not be in the wisdom of men but in the power of God* (1 Corinthians 2:1-5).

It's obvious that Satan does not want our church services to be free. He does not want those who are captive and oppressed to be liberated.

"IS IT OKAY TO PRAY IN TONGUES IN CHURCH?"

"The Spirit of the Lord is upon Me, Because He has anointed Me To preach the gospel to the poor; He has sent Me to heal the brokenhearted, To proclaim liberty to the captives And recovery of sight to the blind, To set at liberty those who are oppressed; (Luke 4:18)

Now the Lord is the Spirit; and where the Spirit of the Lord is, there is liberty (2 Corinthians 3:17).

Stand fast therefore in the liberty by which Christ has made us free, and do not be entangled again with a yoke of bondage (Galatians 5:1)

Let's make our Declaration of Independence from Satan and his hindering spirits. Let's make our Declaration of Dependence on God! Let's stand fast in the liberty in which Christ has made us free! Let's be FREE in our lives and in our church services, and as Paul says in

1 Corinthians 14:40, let's "Let all things be done!"

CONCLUSION

Is it okay to pray in tongues in church?

Yes, it is okay to have the Gifts of the Spirit *as He wills*, such as the Gift of Tongues and Interpretation of Tongues, understanding that the Gift of the Spirit "Tongues" (when God is speaking to us) should be interpreted. If there is no interpreter the Gift should not operate, for no-one would be edified.

Yes, it is okay to have the Gift of Prophecy *as He wills* — and since this operates in a known language, no interpretation is necessary and all will be edified.

Yes, it is also okay to pray and sing in the Spirit *as we will*, when we are speaking to God — ministering to Him as in acts 13:1-3, or praying for others as in Romans 8:26-27, in a church service — no interpretation is necessary. We will not understand what we are saying (1 Corinthians 14:14), however, we should pray that we *may* interpret that we *may* receive edification (1 Corinthians 14:13). We believe that speaking in tongues *as we will* (1 Corinthians 14:15, 18), is our personal prayer language whereby we

"IS IT OKAY TO PRAY IN TONGUES IN CHURCH?"

can minister to the Lord (Acts 13:1-3), give thanks well (1 Corinthians 14:17), and pray for the saints according to the will of God (Romans 8:26-27).

The question "who are we speaking to" answers the question "Is it okay to pray in tongues in church?"

Corporately, when we are speaking to God *as we will*, the answer is yes, and we should pray that we *may* interpret. When God is speaking to us *as He wills*, the answer is yes, and it must be interpreted.

Again, let ALL things be done decently and in order. Tongues, whether they are *as we will* speaking to God, or *as He wills* speaking to us, are both a sign to unbelievers and should not be forbidden (1 Corinthians 14:39-40) as long as they are done decently and in order.

Love is always the answer.

So, we end with our opening scripture…

1 AND THE angel who talked with me came again and awakened me, like a man who is wakened out of his sleep.

2 And said to me, What do you see? I said, I see, and behold, a lampstand all of gold, with its bowl [for oil] on the top of it and its seven lamps on it, and [there are] seven pipes to each of the seven lamps which are upon the top of it.

Conclusion

3 And there are two olive trees by it, one upon the right side of the bowl and the other upon the left side of it [feeding it continuously with oil].

4 So I asked the angel who talked with me, What are these, my lord?

5 Then the angel who talked with me answered me, Do you not know what these are? And I said, No, my lord.

6 Then he said to me, This [addition of the bowl to the candlestick, causing it to yield a ceaseless supply of oil from the olive trees] is the word of the Lord to Zerubbabel, saying, Not by might, nor by power, but by My Spirit [of Whom the oil is a symbol], says the Lord of hosts (Zechariah 4:1-6 AMP).

God showed the prophet Zechariah a lampstand that had a direct connection to two olive trees. The lamps would burn forever because the olive trees supplied oil continuously to the bowl and the pipes supplied oil directly from the bowl to the lamps. This is how our life should be. We need to understand that it is not by our own strength or power, it's by the Holy Spirit within us that we can do all things through Christ (Philippians 4:13).

> 35 Keep your loins girded *and your lamps burning,*
>
> 36 And be like men who are waiting for their master to return home from the marriage feast, so that when he returns from the wedding and comes and knocks, they may open to him immediately (Luke 12:35-36 AMP).

"IS IT OKAY TO PRAY IN TONGUES IN CHURCH?"

If it is truly Him who is greater within us than he that is in the world (1 John 4:4), then the more Holy Spirit we can have within us, the more victorious we will be in life. Both the Gifts of the *Spirit,* designed to guide us and empower us, and the Fruit of the *Spirit,* designed to give us character and strength (Galatians 5:22-23), are "by the Spirit of God." What we need is MORE of the Holy Spirit not less! MORE, MORE, MORE, MORE! We need MORE in our personal lives and we need MORE in our church life! The only way for salvation, healing, deliverance, prosperity, wisdom, miracles, and power to take place is by His Spirit. Let us not remove Him from our services; let us give Him total liberty to accomplish His will for His purpose!

> So he answered and said to me: "This is the word of the Lord to Zerubbabel: *'Not by might nor by power, but by My Spirit,' Says the Lord of hosts* (Zechariah 4:6).

If you have been blessed by this book, received salvation or the Baptism of the Holy Spirit, please take the time to let me know. If you are a pastor and this book has helped encourage you to flow with the power of God in your services it would bless me greatly to know about it. Please write to P.O. Box 1568, Mechanicsville, VA 23116, or e-mail me at pastorjim@mastershouse.net. I would love to hear your testimony. **God bless you!**

BIBLIOGRAPHY

All scriptures referenced are from the New King James Version (NKJV) except as noted.

The New King James Version (NKJV). Nashville: Thomas Nelson. 1982.

Darby, J. N. *1890 Darby Bible* (DARBY). The Holy Scriptures: A new translation from the original languages. Oak Harbor: Logos Research Systems. 1996.

The Amplified Bible (AMP), containing the amplified Old Testament and the amplified New Testament. La Habra, CA: The Lockman Foundation. 1987.

The Holy Bible: *English Standard Version* (ESV). Wheaton: Standard Bible Society. 2001.

International Standard Version New Testament (ISV). Version 1.1. (Print on Demand ed.) Yorba Linda, CA: The Learning Foundation. 2000.

The Holy Bible: *King James Version* (KJV). (electronic ed. of the 1769 edition of the 1611 Authorized Version.) Bellingham WA: Logos Research Systems, Inc. 1995.

The Contemporary English Version (CEV). With Apocrypha., (electronic ed.) Nashville: Thomas Nelson. 1997 c1995

The Holy Bible: *The Good news Translation* (GNT) (2nd ed.) New York: American Bible Society. 1992.

Taylor, K. N. *The living Bible* (TLB), paraphrased. "A compilation of the Scripture paraphrases previously published... under the following titles: Living letters, 1962; Living prophecies, 1965; Living Gospels, 1966; Living Psalms and Proverbs, 1967; Living lessons of life and love, 1968; Living books of Moses, 1969; Living history of Israel, 1970." Wheaton, Ill.: Tyndale House. 1997, c1971.

Peterson, E. H. *The Message* (The Message). The Bible in contemporary language. Colorado Springs, Colo.: NavPress. 2002.

The New American Bible (NABWRNT). Confraternity of Christian Doctrine. Board of Trustees, Catholic Church. National Conference of Catholic Bishops, & United States Catholic Conference. Administrative Board. Translated from the original languages with critical use of all the ancient sources and the revised New Testament. 1996, c1986.

The Holy Bible: *New Living Translation* (NLT). Holy Bible: "Text edition"—Spine. (2nd ed.) Wheaton, Ill.: Tyndale House Publishers. 2004).

Wuest, K. S. *Wuest New Testament* (WUESTNT). The New Testament: An expanded translation. First published in 3 vols., 1956-59, under title: Expanded translation of the Greek New Testament. Grand Rapids, MI: Eerdmans. 1997, c1961.

ABOUT THE AUTHOR

Pastor Jim Langlois (pronounced "lang-wah"), a.k.a. "Captain Charismatic" to many children, has served as an Assistant Pastor, Helps Ministry Director, Local Outreach Director, Children's Ministry Director, Bible School Teacher, Video Department Director, and Drummer in the Praise Band, for over 25 years in Richmond, VA. Through serving the Lord in these many ways, he has come to know a deep understanding of the vision and purpose in ministry. He began ministering to children in January 1982. He also directed a local church's outreach program called "Richmond Reach-Out." During nine years of directing more than 35 inner-city crusades over 10,000 souls came to Christ! He has ministered in International Children's Crusades in Russia, Africa, Jamaica, Guatemala, and Trinidad, where combined well over 50,000 souls have come to know the Lord. He has directed many children's workers seminars throughout the

"IS IT OKAY TO PRAY IN TONGUES IN CHURCH?"

United States and abroad with a vision to raise-up children's workers with the right heart, purpose, and tools that they need. The Captain is the author of "the Captain's Rap," two songs that teach children the books of the Bible from memory. These songs have literally gone around the world! He also has two other full length music CD's teaching kids important principles in the Word of God. He has directed and co-written a Bible School for Children called MKPFM, "The Master's Kids Preparation for Ministry" Bible School.

January 1st, 2003 He began "MKEA," The Master's Kids Evangelistic Association, Inc., www.mkea.org. Within the first year traveling and holding family evangelistic crusades and children's workers conferences, he saw over 1000 kids and adults respond to altar calls for salvation, healing, and a closer relationship to the Lord! On January 11th, 2004, he pioneered "The Master's House," a church in Ashland VA. with the vision *"Building the Family of God."* He has received both his Bachelors and Master's in Theology through Life Christian University, of which The Master's House is an extension campus. The web-site for The Master's House is www.mastershouse.net.